CW00952397

Superperformance Stocks

An Investment Strategy for
the Individual Investor
Based on the 4-Year Political Cycle

by Richard S. Love

To the Individual Investor,

Whose Security Investments Are Manipulated by
His Government, Whipsawed by Wall Street
Professionals, and Dominated by Institutions.

*Superperformance Stocks: An Investment Strategy for the Individual
Investor Based on the 4-Year Poiitical Cycle* by Richard S. Love
Copyright © 1977 by Richard S. Love

info@parkerpub.co

Library of Congress Cataloging in Publication Data
Love, Richard S
    Superperformance Stocks.

    1. Stocks. 2. Investments. 3. Speculation

Special thanks go out to the guy who makes this possible

I can´t say what a lucky guy I am to met you

Acknowledgments

My sincere thanks to Oscar Collier for his valuable advice, encouragement and assistance, and to Darrell Husted for his important editorial contributions.

The Securities Research Company, 208 Newbury Street, Boston, Mass., 02116, was kind enough to permit me to reproduce their charts for use in this book. I acknowledge a debt of gratitude to them.

Contents

Part III

Which Stocks Should You Buy?

Charts

Tables

Part I
The Search
for a
Successful Investment
Strategy

Chapter 1
Buy to Keep or Buy to Sell?

A well-known investment adviser was interviewed by a national magazine a few years ago and asked to sum up the investment philosophy he would recommend for the person who still has twenty or thirty years in which to buy stocks. He advised buying to keep rather than buying to sell.

A financial columnist stated in another magazine: "The conventional wisdom of stocks being bought and put away for the long-term has been so discredited that there is no need to dwell on it here."

Here are two financial advisers with two opposing opinions. Which one is right? Since the statements were made prior to the devastating 1973-1974 bear market when almost all stock prices declined severely—their steepest declines since 1929—and during a period of increasing pessimism concerning the national economy, the investment adviser who said that long-term investment has been discredited appears to be right. During that year stocks declined in value about $500 billion. However, an investor who bought IBM, or Xerox, or Eastman Kodak, or any of a dozen or so other growth companies in the 1950s or early 1960s and has held the shares has certainly done very well.

But there are at least two problems. First, would an individual investor have done as well buying and holding even the most consistently strong stocks as by buying when prices were depressed and selling when prices appeared high? I believe that the evidence on long-term charts such as those in this book clearly indicates that better results are usually obtained by timely selling, and then repurchasing the stock or a more suitable one after a bear market has run its course. Second, the best reason for selling when a stock turns weak is simply that many stocks never come back, and others take many years to return to earlier price levels.

The Concept of Growth

Growth is a word that has triggered off the purchase of billions of dollars' worth of stock by millions of Americans for many years. As far back as the 1920s the belief was widespread that the way to invest was to buy the stock of a growing company and to hold it. During the 1930s some investors presumably had second thoughts. But the mania for growth reached another peak in the 1960s; the price/earnings levels of most stocks in 1961, for example, were even higher than in 1929.

But although rapid growth is a highly desirable feature to find in a company, the relationship of a stock's price to the company's rate of growth must be realistic. Investors have paid high prices for growth that was to occur many, many years in the future, and which often never happened at all. Moreover, growth stocks eventually reach maturity and the rate of growth slows down.

Too many investors confuse growth stocks with growth companies. A company may have rapidly growing sales and earnings over a period of ten years or more, but if the stock was extremely overpriced at the beginning of that ten-year period because investors were looking forward to future growth, the price of the stock might rise very little, if at all. Communications Satellite Corporation, or Comsat, is such an example. When the company was organized, in 1964, its stock was sold to the public for twenty dollars a share. There was great public enthusiasm about the "growth" expected for this stock, and its price quickly rose to over seventy dollars a share. This happened several years before the company reported any earnings. Although profits were reported in 1968 and have been steadily rising since then, the stock's price has fluctuated widely between eighty-five and twenty-three dollars a share as recently as 1974 and 1975. In other words, the stock's price back in 1964 completely discounted an entire decade of growth for the company. Investors are not willing to pay as much now for a company and its prospects as they were ten years ago. So although the nation may grow and expand, and an individual company may grow and expand, this does not necessarily mean that the company's stock must rise in price.

In recent years there have been hundreds of companies reporting expanding sales and increasing earnings, but declining stock prices. In numerous cases the combination of rising earnings but declining stock price is a long-term trend that has lasted a decade or longer, and indicates that investors are not as willing to pay as much for earnings as they once were. With inflation pushing up the yields available from bonds and certificates of deposit, many investors are satisfied with placing their money there rather than in lower-yielding and riskier stocks.

The concept of growth has been shaken even more by the increasingly cyclical nature of the American economy, the result of the higher rate of inflation in recent years, which has in turn been caused by the numerous big-spending programs favored by Washington politicians. Big programs require big money, and if the funds squeezed out of the taxpayers are insufficient, the Washington managers in effect create or borrow whatever additional money is required to pay the bills of the government.

So what does this mean for the individual investor? It means that the concept of steady upward-and-onward "growth" is shaky. Companies might grow, but their stocks often go through periods of severe price distortion, sometimes being greatly undervalued, then overvalued two or three years later.

The Cyclical Approach

Instead of just looking for "growth," there is a better, more rewarding approach to achieving stock market profits, which I discovered by studying the patterns

§

made by stock prices plotted on twelve-year charts. These charts reveal that the vast majority of stock prices move in four-year cycles of strength and weakness, with strength occurring prior to and weakness occurring after presidential elections. The strength or weakness in stock prices reflects the mass optimism or mass pessimism of investors as they anticipate higher or lower earnings for companies.

I nvestors are not the only people who are alternately optimistic and pessimistic. Our economy is cyclical in part because buyers, too, act in waves of optimism and pessimism. When people are pessimistic concerning their future, they delay making big purchases such as houses and automobiles; but when they all become optimistic and do their buying at the same time, shortages are created and prices and wages are raised. Because of the shortages, and to beat rising prices, businessmen-retailers, wholesalers, manufacturers—place larger orders than they really need, so their inventories grow. But the new higher prices cause hesitation on the part of the buyers. So buying—and business-slow down and mass pessimism gradually replaces optimism.

Just as the history of stock prices can be determined very quickly by simply glancing at the picture record portrayed on long-term stock charts, the reason for volatile stock action at a certain time can be determined by reviewing the financial magazines and newspapers of the period. Thus related to the historical record, long-term charts become a picture of economic history, recording booms and recessions, inflation and international crises. The charts are a reflection of mass behavior patterns, as millions of investors react in panic or enthusiasm to the news of the day.

Will the cyclical four-year stock-price pattern continue? Yes, because it is closely related to the presidential term of office, and as long as the term of office remains four years the same pattern is likely to persist.

We live in the Age of the Big Spender-the politician

who loves to spend other people's money for every imaginable cause ranging from foreign aid to Frisbee research. Washington's big spending is the primary reason for the large hidden tax—inflation—that afflicts all of us. Until the Federal Government gets its spending under control, if it ever does, the problem of inflation and economic instability, with its booms and recessions, spiraling prices and business failures, will be with us. For the investor this can spell opportunity or disaster, depending on each individual's insight.

Evaluate the Political Climate

Many thousands of pages have been written about fundamental analysis and technical approaches to common stock investment. Comparatively little attention has been given to the importance of political influences, particularly as they affect the timing of purchases. But it is in Washington that most of the important decisions are made that will cause you to lose or make money in the stock market. Washington policymakers will decide if there will be a budget deficit or a possible surplus; Washington policymakers will decide if there will be any changes in federal taxes; and Washington policymakers will decide if there is to be a monetary contraction or expansion. It would be a big mistake, when deciding on stock purchases or sales, to ignore policies being formulated by the federal government.

Many made-in-Washington decisions are influenced by the necessities of running for political office. Every four years there is a presidential election, and the White House incumbent knows that he or his political party's nominee will stand a better chance of winning if the nation is prosperous at the time of the election. Politicians consider the "pocketbook" issue to be the most important of all.

The significance to the investor is that he can plan on the country being economically strong during an election year, and since rising stock prices are associated with a strengthening economy, he can expect rising stock prices during the two-year period prior to the election.

But after the election there is no longer this concern, and another problem begins to receive increased attention: inflation. The booming economy of the presidential election year aggravates the inflation problem, so after the election—and sometimes just prior to election day—steps are taken to attempt to slow down the inflation rate. These restrictive moves by the Federal Reserve Board may include increases in the rediscount rate, increases in the reserve requirements of member banks, and increases in margin requirements.

Such steps are usually effective in gradually slowing the nation's economy. The stock market reacts to the new policies more quickly and begins to decline, a slide that might last as long as two years.

The signal for the end of the stock market decline comes when Washington begins to adopt policies to fight the recession that is developing. These steps include new expansive measures by the Federal Reserve Board, and fiscal policies of increased government spending and tax cuts. These new economic stimuli will not stop the slide in stock prices immediately, since deep pessimism is the prevailing mood at such times. But after a delay of several weeks or months, the market will have a selling climax and reverse its direction, though the nation's economy is likely to continue weakening for several more months.

The upswing in the direction of stock prices following the selling climax is the beginning of a new price cycle, which will continue bullish for about two or two and a half years, through the next presidential election.

That, in general, is what investors should expect because of the political cycle and its effect on the nation's economy and stock prices. Federal monetary policies, moreover, are likely to become more political rather than less, since there are persistent efforts in the

Congress to bring the Federal Reserve Board's power under the control of congressional committees. The result would probably be a still greater increase in monetary inflation.

The significance of these political-economic decisions and numerous others emanating from Washington is that they have a very pervasive influence on the psychology of investors as well as on the availability and cost of money.

Before making purchases, then, be sure to assess the prevailing political economic climate. Review the President's annual budget message to Congress to determine whether he expects to be able to balance the budget or, instead, expects increased government spending and another large deficit. The administration's policies determine largely whether or not the national economy will be stimulated or slowed.

Monetary indicators turn up before there is a business upswing, and stock should be bought while business is still going down. One highly regarded investment advisory service has stated that every one of their major buy signals since 1945 was given before the trough in the business cycle. Toward the end of the boom period you should be prepared to sell stocks if weakness develops in monetary indicators, which occurs prior to the peaks in the stock market and in business.

Is Institutional Investment Strategy Changing?

On February 9, 1966, the Dow Jones industrial average reached 1001.11. Almost nine years later, in October 1974, the Dow Jones industrial average was as low as 573, indicating that investors who had bought and held stocks were not faring well. Of the thirty large companies that comprise the Dow Jones industrials, twenty-eight were selling at lower prices in October 1974 than they had been in February 1966.

Some of the largest institutional investors have

started to move away from the one-decision growth-stock investment strategy, the buy-and-hold approach to investing. The 1973-74 bear market evidently brought about this change in the thinking of some portfolio managers. In 1974 *Forbes Magazine* interviewed a bank senior vice-president who supervised $16 billion worth of pension money. *Forbes* quoted him as saying: "We didn't feel that we were smart enough to buy and sell these stocks when they were going through periods of over-valuation and then buy them back when they went down." But now, he said, "When the degree of valuation becomes excessive, we will be more willing to share our holdings with new enthusiasts." So it appears that at least some large institutional investors are rethinking their investment strategy and will use an intermediate term buy-sell-buy approach. This investment philosophy will cause even larger swings in stock prices, which creates greater opportunities for individual investors who are alert enough to buy and sell the right stocks at the right time.

Stock-Price Cycles

If the buy-and-hold approach to investing is unsatisfactory, as it often has been, then the alternative is to buy for resale, preferably at a much higher price. But how are the ideal times to purchase and sell stocks determined? The answer is found in the cyclical pattern of stock prices, a pattern that has developed over the past few decades.

Cycles in stock prices can be readily identified on long-term charts of market averages, which are valuable for determining the trend of stock prices in general. Cycles can also be identified on individual stock charts. Chart 1 portrays the record of six market averages, including the Dow Jones industrial average. The cyclical pattern traced by the Dow Jones industrials clearly reveals the periods of price weakness as well as the long periods of advancing stock prices. From 1949 to 1965 the Dow Jones industrial average was in a general up-trend, interrupted about every four years by sharp declines. After 1965 the general trend has been sideways, but still interrupted by bear markets. The patterns of strength and weakness can be traced not only on charts of market averages but also on the charts of many stocks such as Ford Motor, shown in Chart 2, and Metromedia, shown in Chart 3.

The chart of the Dow Jones industrials shows that bear markets occurred in 1949, 1953, 1957, 1960, 1962, 1966,1969-70, and 1973-74, with periods of greater strength between those years. The twelve-year chart of Ford shows the price declines of 1966, 1969-70, and 1974-75 and the greater strength between those bear market phases. The chart of Metromedia, a much smaller company, reveals greater volatility in the price of its stock, but the price history shows the weakness in 1966, 1969-70, and 1974-75, with strong rallies between the periods of weakness. As illustrated by the long-term charts, it is apparent that stock-price cycles are not only real, but are also quite consistent in the length of their intervals between bear market lows.

Reading the Long-Term Charts

The long-term charts in this book, developed by Securities Research Company, 208 Newbury Street, Boston, Massachusetts 02116, are designed so that when the Price-Range bars and the Earnings line coincide, this indicates that the price is at fifteen times earnings. When the price is above the earnings line, the ratio of price to earnings is greater than fifteen times earnings; when below, it is less. These charts permit an investor to determine quickly whether the P/E ratio of a company is expanding or contracting, and by how much.

CHART 1. PRESIDENTIAL ELECTIONS AND STOCK PRICES

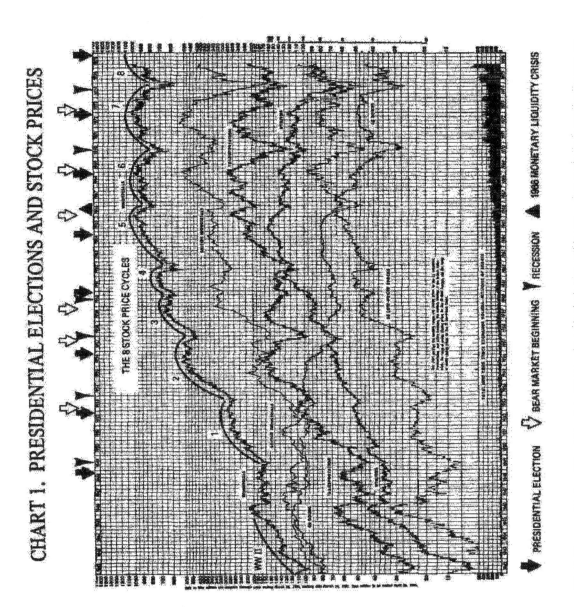

▶ PRESIDENTIAL ELECTION   ⇩ BEAR MARKET BEGINNING   ⅄ RECESSION   ▲ 1966 MONETARY LIQUIDITY CRISIS

The black arrows at the top of the chart indicate the date of presidential elections. White arrows show the beginnings of bear markets. By comparing the arrow with the line chart showing the monthly highs and lows of the Dow Jones industrials, the pattern of weak stock prices following presidential elections can be seen. Periods of recession are also indicated.

Chart by Securities Research Company.

12

CHART 2. FORD MOTOR

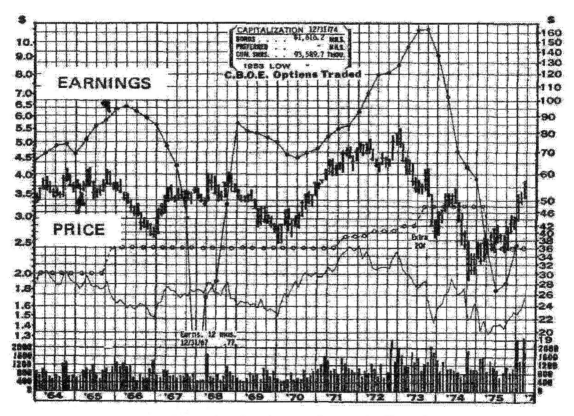

This twelve-year chart clearly shows the periodic price declines in Ford common stock. From a high above 60 in late 1965, the price dropped to below 40 in December 1966. By late 1968 the stock had regained its earlier levels, but a new decline began in November 1968 at 60. The decline ended in early 1970 at 37. A rise then carried the price above 80 in January 1973, but the stock dropped to below 30 during the 1973-74 bear market.

Chart by Securities Research Company

W

CHART 3. METROMEDIA

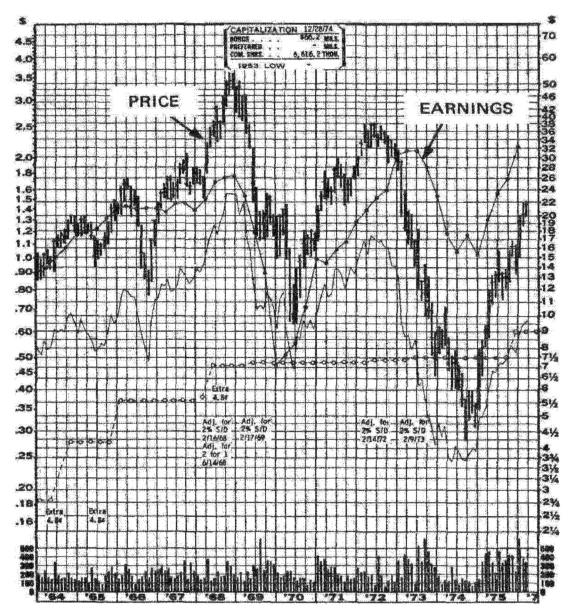

The twelve-year chart of this radio, television, and advertising company shows the cyclical nature of its stock. From about 26 in early 1966, the price dropped to below 12 in late 1966. By late 1968 the price had risen to above 50, but by mid-1970 had fallen to 9'/z. By mid-1972 the price was back up to 38, but then dropped to 4% in September 1974. From that level it again rallied sharply during 1975 and 1976.

Chart by Securities Research Company

Being Wrong Can Be Painful

The 1973-74 bear market made many investors painfully aware of the fact that they can be seriously hurt if they hold stocks while many other stockholders are selling in panic. During the 1974 plunge, even fire and casualty insurance companies were forced into heavy selling from their portfolios. These companies need a surplus usually about equal to 25 percent of the net premiums that they write. But the fire and casualty companies had a large portion of their surplus invested in stocks, and several lost as much as 80 percent of their surplus. They were therefore forced to sell stocks and losses were severe. The market value decline in the stock portfolios of the fire and casualty insurance companies during the 1973-74 bear market has been estimated at several billion dollars.

There are other disadvantages to buying and holding. Some stocks never come back after plunging. Others take many years to return to their earlier levels. Even General Motors, usually considered to be among the strongest of companies, has had its stock sell at prices far below those reached in 1965. This has also been true of other mature companies. American Telephone and Telegraph, for instance, reached a high of 75 in 1964 and has been below that price ever since. DuPont has not regained its 1965 high, nor has U. S. Steel regained its 1959 high, or Alcoa its 1956 level. There are numerous other examples.

But the biggest disadvantage is that bear markets are injurious to your health and might even kill you, though no warning to that effect is printed on stock certificates. During the severe sell-offs of the 1969-70 bear market a radio commentator reported that the rate of heart attacks had increased, and this was believed to be related to the plunge in stock prices.

Mental anguish is a severe problem associated with bear markets that most investors do not even consider until they are hopelessly entangled in the continuing dilemma of whether to sell and what to sell and when to sell, while the value of their investments plunges between 10:00 A.M. and 3:30 P.M. on five days of the week-all the while hoping that their stocks will go back up to their purchase prices so that they can at least get out even. During such periods there is almost a nationwide sigh of relief when the closing bell rings at the stock exchange. And the arrival of weekends is a reason for wild jubilation, for stock prices do not decline then, and so for two whole glorious days you cannot be hurt.

Living in this kind of constant tension, fear, almost panic that the impersonal stock market will decree that an individual's worth will be so many thousands or millions of dollars less on Friday than on the previous Monday takes its toll, and a number of lives per year.

I knew a man who had built a thriving business over the years, but who decided to retire when he was in his late sixties. He sold his business at a good price and invested the money in various "growth" stocks recommended by his broker. Within months the market had started on a steep decline, ending in the severe sell-offs of June and October 1962. My friend's stocks declined in value to a fraction of their purchase price. He developed hypertension and died of a heart attack two years later. Most investors would not be as severely affected as this businessman was, but plunging stock prices affect just about everybody who owns stocks—at least twenty-four million people.

The Disadvantages of the Buy-Sell-Buy Approach

The disadvantages of the buy-sell-buy approach to investing are apparent: Commissions must be paid on purchases and sales; income taxes must be paid on capital gains, and, in addition, the investor might not feel confident about his ability to sell and buy back stocks at the right time. But in spite of these negative aspects, the advantages of buying and selling in accord with stock-price cycles are so great that in most cases the profits to be obtained will vastly exceed the capital gains taxes to be paid. The stock-price history of the past few decades reveals that investors who have the talent for buying and selling stocks at the right times would have been much more successful than investors who merely purchased and held stocks. To answer our initial question, the financial columnist who advised the purchase of stocks for resale rather than to keep is correct.

Part II
When Should You Buy Stocks?

Chapter 2
Business Cycles

Stock-price cycles are usually related to cycles in the national economy. Companies exist to make money. Those that are not profitable do not remain on the national scene for many years. Stocks are purchased or sold because investors become optimistic or pessimistic about company earnings. Company earnings are usually dependent on the state of the nation's economy.

Business cycles result from fluctuations in the economic activity of a nation. They consist of a phase of economic expansion followed by contraction. Revival of business activity emerges from the contraction and becomes the expansion of the next cycle.

The economy of the United States has experienced periods of decline throughout the nation's history. The National Bureau of Economic Research has identified more than thirty periods of business contraction, dating as far back as 1834. In European countries cycles of business have been traced back to earlier periods. According to some economists, the accumulation of large amounts of capital appears to be the key factor in the development of business cycles. Fluctuations in the production of durable goods, such as automobiles and capital equipment for businesses, have been much more severe than in the production of nondurables. This is because durables are frequently purchased on credit. They are also postponable items. Thus, purchases tend to be bunched together in periods of optimisim and easy credit.

An expansion phase of a business cycle may originate from increased spending by business, consumers, or the government. In this phase banks have excess reserves. But as the boom advances, more money is required to finance it. Eventually excess reserves disappear and credit sources dry up. Commercial banks can create more deposits only if they receive additional reserves. Competition for loans drives interest rates up, and on some occasions money has not been obtainable at any price.

Eventually a slowing down of the boom begins to take place. Production costs rise rapidly; sales stop increasing; some consumer items become oversupplied; overoptimism is replaced by doubt and a reluctance to go further into debt. The momentum of the business expansion finally falters and begins to reverse itself. To a large extent, then, business cycles result from widespread feelings of optimism or pessimism, as well as from the cost of and availability of credit.

Tight money policies will slow a boom. But easy money policies are less effective in pulling an economy out of a slump, although low interest rates and readily available credit will help. Government spending also will be beneficial, but investment spending is the most important factor. The business contraction can sometimes last for years.

According to business cycle theory, a ceiling is established for cyclical upswings when full employment is reached; further growth is not possible. Cycle theory also presupposes that a floor is established when excess production capacity has been worked off. The expectation of profit is the strong motivating force behind investment decisions. If corporation managements believe that a good profit can be obtained from new manufacturing facilities, they will probably decide to build the facilities. But the cost of money, labor, raw materials, and equipment must be sufficiently low to justify the investment. And a market for the products must be anticipated. If these conditions are met, new business investment will occur and a business cycle upswing will take place.

Stock prices anticipate the decline in business by turning down before business begins to decline, just as stock prices anticipate upturns in the business cycle several months in advance. Since World War II severe reactions in stock prices have occurred approximately every four years, and the bottom of the price decline has occurred most often during the second year following a presidential election but also late in the first year following the election. The beginning of the decline has varied from less than a month following the election to approximately thirteen months later.

Chapter 3
Washington Policies

Movements in stock prices, like business cycles, are forecast by political developments and are affected by actions related to the election of a United States President every four years.

The key to correctly anticipating the direction of the national economy and stock prices can be found in Washington. The President and other Washington politicians and bureaucrats have gained extensive control over the American economy since the Depression of the 1930s.

Anyone who has watched the maneuvers of the Washington Establishment for a long time is aware of the incessant desire of its politicians and bureaucrats to control or manipulate most aspects of American life. They are involved in the nation's education and housing, its transportation, and much of its industry. America's energy is to a large extent under their control, as is foreign commerce. They also exercise a considerable degree of control over the nation's economy through their manipulation of the money supply, and through the taxing and spending authority of the Federal Government.

The severe economic Depression of the 1930s gave an important boost to government interference in the economy, interference that has been most closely associated with the theories of the British economist John Maynard Keynes.

Central to Keynesian economics is the belief that the government should stimulate spending if there is a tendency to unemployment, and that it should restrain spending if there is a trend toward increased inflation. Keynesian economists believe that the government can regulate spending by varying the level of taxes and subsidies, thereby altering the amount of purchasing power in the hands of consumers.

Investment spending can be regulated by varying the tax rate on profits and by controlling the availability and cost of credit. The inducement to invest could thus be controlled to the extent that it depended on the prospective net rate of return after taxes. Thus, the Keynesian economists concluded, the selection of different techniques for regulating demand would depend on the goals that the government is pursuing.

This power to slow down or speed up the level of economic activity can lead to many abuses, among them the possibility that the economy might be stimulated when it serves the purpose of the individuals who have control. Too much stimulation can be destructive, since it can trigger serious inflation and result in a severe recession. But these concerns sometimes seem to be of secondary importance when compared with the necessity of winning elections with votes bought with the taxpayer's own money.

Economic Control Through Fiscal and Monetary Policies

Although most investors are probably aware that business activity has moved in patterns of boom and bust, prosperity and recession for hundreds of years, they are perhaps less aware of the specific influences that Washington exercises in determining the timing of these phases.

The effects of federal fiscal policy, which is the government's spending and taxing authority, and federal monetary policy, which is its control over the nation's money, have been well established. For over a decade changes in federal monetary policy, for example, have preceded changes in the level of the nation's economic activity. Monetary authorities have taken steps to increase the availability of credit and to lower its costs when the nation has been in or close to a recession. They have taken steps to decrease the availability of credit and to increase its cost when inflation has been a serious threat to the country's stability. These steps have usually preceded, and probably influenced, the resulting changes in the primary trend of stock prices.

Changes in monetary policy are made to control inflation by switching from a policy of monetary ease to one of monetary restraint, and to fight recession by switching from monetary restraint to monetary ease. But timing of the policy change is sometimes affected by political considerations. Policies of monetary restraint, for example, can be delayed until after presidential elections so that a plunging stock market and a deteriorating economy will not affect an incumbent President's chances of re-election. A comparison of long-term charts of stock prices with the dates of monetary policy changes, federal fiscal actions, and the schedule of presidential elections reveals that there have been occasions when federal fiscal and monetary policies were modified in order to accommodate political ambitions. The importance of this information to the individual investor is not only that it can help him to avoid some stock market losses, but that it can assist him in planning a strategy for timing the purchase and sale of stocks.

Follow the Political Cycle

Since it is possible to anticipate periods when federal authorities can be expected to take actions detrimental to stock prices, and also to anticipate times when favorable action is expected, an investment strategy based on these political decisions can be successful.

The principal influence that will determine when you should buy and sell stocks is the political cycle, the four-year presidential term. There is a desire on the part of the politicians whose policies determine national economic trends to have the confidence of the voters at election time, and the most important influence in creating confidence is prosperity. To have general prosperity, then, the business cycle must be in a phase in which the national economy is improving, with production and employment increasing and wages rising, resulting in a general feeling of optimism. It is also during this phase of the business cycle that stock prices are rising, with the primary trend of the stock market moving upward.

But as the upward surge in the national economy continues, prices and wages also accelerate and inflation becomes a bigger problem. So, after the election, when there is no longer a political angle to consider, anti-inflation policies are initiated, which gradually bring about a shift to the business cycle's next phase: contraction. Preceding the slowdown in the economy will be a downturn in the stock market's primary trend, the basic direction of stock prices over a period of months, interrupted only briefly by temporary dips or rallies.

Inflationary Policies

It is more than coincidental that economic booms occur regularly during presidential years and that recessions occur in years between presidential elections. Business cycles cannot be eliminated, but their timing can be affected considerably by the fiscal and monetary policies of the Federal Government.

Fiscal policy, the taxing and spending power of the Federal Government, is the most powerful influence affecting the nation's economy. The overall size of federal appropriations is very important, as are the budget deficits (shown in Chart 4). The deficits requirs the Treasury to borrow funds in the open market in competition with business. If these funds cannot be readily obtained in the open market, the Federal Reserve Board purchases the Treasury's securities, thereby

CHART 4. FEDERAL BUDGET DEFICITS AND SURPLUSES

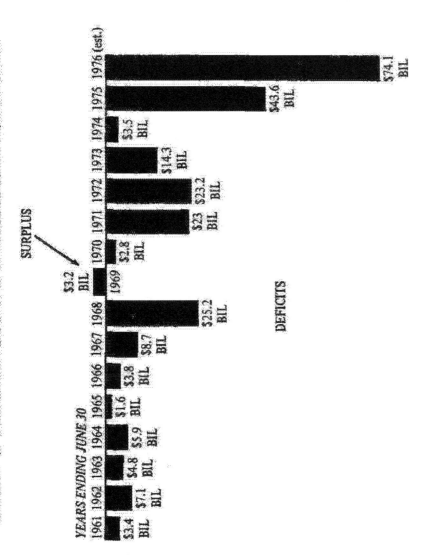

The major reason for inflation and high interest rates is the Federal Government's demand for large amounts of credit because of budget deficits. The problem is particularly acute when the nation's economy is strong and businesses also require large amounts of credit. The President is not entirely to blame for large budget deficits. Big-spending congressmen are equally at fault, along with lower federal income because of recession. The year 1969 is the only one since 1960 that has had a budget surplus.

29

"monetizing" the debt, another way of saying that they are adding new money to the nation's money supply.

A study correlating periods of inflation with subsequent large federal budget deficits was published in the July/August 1974 edition of the *Financial Analysts Journal.* The author, Mr. Jesse Levin, determined that the periods of strong inflation follow periods of large federal deficits, with a lag of $1\,{}^1/2$ to $2\,{}^1/2$ years. He concluded: "Every increase in the federal budget deficit since 1945 has invariably resulted in a corresponding increase in the acceleration of inflation; and every surplus has produced a slow down in this rate. There have been no exceptions."

Large deficits in the federal budget also complicate the Federal Reserve Board's responsibility for maintaining a consistent noninflationary monetary policy. When the federal budget has a deficit, as it has had continuously for more than a decade, the U. S. Treasury must borrow. In addition, a host of other federal agencies created by Congress also make demands for credit. The Export-Import Bank, the Federal Home Loan Banks, the Federal Land Banks, and the Environmental Financing Authority, to name a few, do not have their credit demands revealed in the budget. The result is that the Federal Reserve is under constant pressure to expand the money supply.

When the Federal Government spends billions of dollars more than it receives in taxes, it is necessary to finance the deficit. To do this the U. S. Treasury sells bonds to buyers who will underwrite the big federal spending, which will be the cause of more inflation, and which will reduce, ironically, the real value of the bonds being purchased by the buyers.

Economic Planning vs. Political Reality

Until recent decades a balanced national budget was considered desirable. But the Great Depression of the

1930s and Keynesian economics introduced a new attitude toward large-scale government spending. Many politicians and economists became convinced that the attainment of full employment was more desirable than a balanced budget.

World War II caused massive government spending for military purposes and the accumulation of purchasing power by businesses and individuals. Following the war, Congress passed the Employment Act of 1946, which stated that it was the continuing policy and responsibility of the Federal Government to promote maximum employment, production, and purchasing power. It was assumed that fiscal and monetary policies would be used to attain these objectives.

By the 1960s this approach had gained widespread acceptance among liberal economists and politicians. The arguments by economists favoring the use of fiscal action to control the nation's economy are that increases in government spending add directly to demand for goods and service, and that reductions in tax rates increase disposable income, thereby increasing demand. Both of these actions have a multiplier effect.

Economists also assumed that an overheated national economy could be cooled down by reducing federal spending and increasing taxes. But this theory collided with hard political reality. Politicians are quick to spend money and reduce taxes, but it is usually very difficult to convince them that the opposite actions—less spending and increased taxes—are sometimes necessary to slow inflation. The unpleasant chore of slowing the economy has been left to the Federal Reserve Board, which effectively slows the economy by tightening credit.

So, while fiscal policies have been particularly useful in stimulating the nation's economy when it need stimulating, responsibility has fallen upon the monetary policymakers, the Federal Reserve Board, to take steps necessary to combat inflation. The Fed accomplishes this through its control over reserve requirements—the amount of money that member banks must hold in reserve as a percentage of deposits—and the discount rate, which is the interest rate charged member banks to borrow from the Federal Reserve. Since increases in the discount rate have the effect of forcing up other interest rates, borrowing by business is discouraged. Decreases in the discount rate, on the other hand, force interest rates down and make borrowing more attractive.

The Fed can also act to peg interbank loans, called federal funds, at desired levels, and can also take action to increase or decrease stock margin requirements, which affect the potential buying power for securities.

Federal Monetary Policy and Stock Prices

There has been a strong correlation between declining stock prices and restrictive policies by the Federal Reserve, and also between rising stock prices and Fed policies of monetary ease. The discount rate was increased repeatedly during the 1973-74 bear market. But the Fed switched to a policy of monetary ease by lowering the discount rate in December 1974 and January 1975.

During 1927 the Federal Reserve Board had an easy-money policy that contributed to heavy stock market speculation. Bank credit expanded and the commercial banks overextended themselves in loans for stock purchases. The Fed slowly began restrictive action by moderately raising discount rates in early 1928 and again in 1929. Also in 1929 it threatened to refuse re-discount privileges to banks having excessive loans based on securities for collateral.

At that time the Federal Reserve lacked the authority to slow stock market speculation. It was not until after the 1929 crash that the Fed was given authority to set margin requirements.

Do Not Be Misled by Short Term Money Trends

One word of warning: It is possible for an investor to be misled if he attempts to follow weekly trends in the money stock figures, since there is considerable fluctuation from week to week. The Federal Reserve does not have the tools to control movements in money with precision over the short term. A more accurate approach would probably be to accept the stated intention of the Federal Reserve as described by the Fed's spokesmen. Federal Reserve policy is often spelled out in speeches and press conferences by the Board's chairman and other members. In the past, these public statements have been accurate indicators of whether the Fed was moving toward a tighter or easier monetary policy. For example, late in 1968 the Federal Reserve Board stated publicly that it intended to squeeze inflation from the economy. This occurred while stock prizes were still rising strongly. Following the 1966 period of tight money, the Federal Reserve announced that it was taking steps to make money more readily available. However, although these steps were publicized, the market was quite slow in reacting to the signals,

Chapter 4
The Political Cycles

The political cycle, the four-year presidential term of office, has been responsible for the development over the past three decades of a four-year cycle in stock prices. The pattern had its inception during Franklin D. Roosevelt's term of office in the mid-1930s, but the domination of the national economy by the demands of World War II prevented the cycle from developing fully until the postwar period.

Chart 5 shows the durations of stock price cycles since the 1940s. Presidential elections were held during the first week of November in 1948, 1952, 1956, 1960, 1964, 1968, and 1972. There were declining stock markets that bottomed out in 1949, 1953, 1957, 1960, 1962, 1966, 1970, and 1974. Of these dates, the only one not in a normal cycle is 1960, which was a presidential election year. The weak national economy and declining stock market played significant roles in the election results that year. All of the bear market bottoms except 1960 occurred within two years after each election.

Since 1949 there have been seven complete cycles in the primary trend of stock prices, as revealed on the long-term charts of six stock averages. The beginning and ending months, and the duration of each cycle, are shown in Table 1. Some bear market troughs were characterized by "double bottoms," during which prices plunged a second time following an initial rebound. Three double bottoms are listed (October and December 1957, June and October 1962, October and December 1974) because at least one stock average recorded its bottom during one month while other averages recorded their lowest levels during another month.

Table 1

Cycle	Trough Date	Length of Cycle (Trough to Trough)

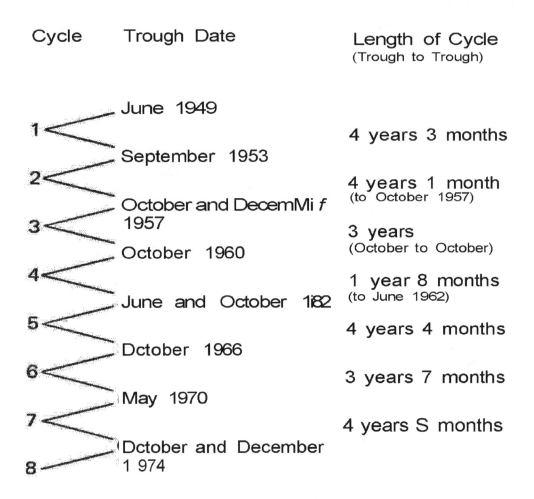

1 June 1949

4 years 3 months

2 September 1953

4 years 1 month
(to October 1957)

3 October and DecemMi *f* 1957

3 years
(October to October)

4 October 1960

1 year 8 months
(to June 1962)

5 June and October 1962

4 years 4 months

6 Dctober 1966

3 years 7 months

7 May 1970

4 years S months

8 Dctober and December 1 974

Prior to 1960 the bear market lows occurred during the year following a presidential election; after 1960 they have occurred in the second year after each election; that is, the year of midterm congressional elections. Since the trough was reached in October in half of the bear markets, it is a great temptation to conclude, based on time patterns, that the next big opportunity for stock purchases could be in October 1978.

CHART 5. DURATIONS OF STOCK PRICE CYCLES

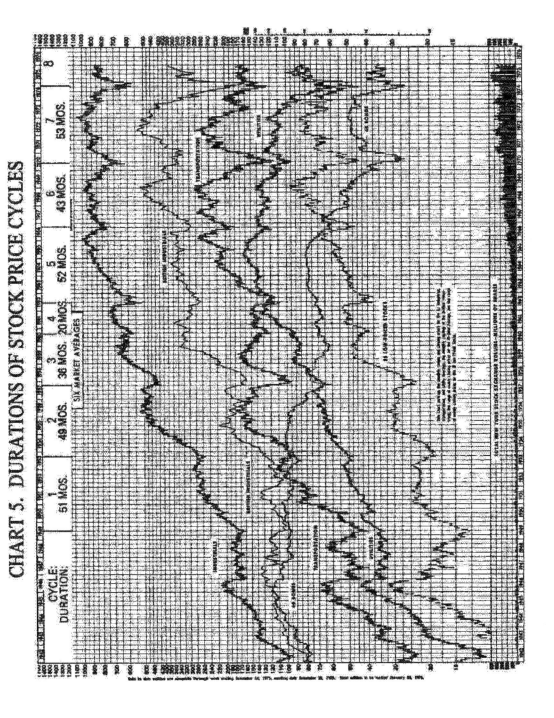

Since 1948 every period between presidential elections has had a bear market in stocks. In 1960 there was an "extra" bear market. The top price bars on the chart are of the Dow Jones industrial average. Periods shown are between bear market troughs.

Chart by Securities Research Company

37

The bear market that occurred during the 1960 presidential election year probably has had an important and lasting influence on the timing of Federal Reserve monetary policies. The 1960 bear market reached its bottom just a few days before the election, timing that seemed almost designed to have maximum impact against the incumbents who were running. Following a $12 billion federal budget deficit in fiscal year 1959, President Elsenhower was determined to leave office with a balanced national budget. A policy of fiscal restraint was adopted and fiscal year 1960 had a rare budget surplus. In addition, the Federal Reserve Board had a restrictive monetary policy. The results included credit restraints, higher interest rates, a mild recession, a decline in stock prices of 17 percent, and a loss of the election by Richard M. Nixon to John F. Kennedy by .1 of 1 percent of the vote. The economic policies of the Elsenhower Administration and the restrictive policies of the Federal Reserve were cited as among the principal reasons for the Republican loss.

In order to conclude that there will be in the future a cycle pattern consisting of a strong presidential-election-year economy with strong stock prices, and a period between elections with a weak national economy and declining stock prices, it is necessary to anticipate whether U. S. Presidents will act in their own self-interest and in the interest of their political party, or whether they will disregard this and take actions, as President Eisenhower did in 1960, that may help the opposition party to elect its candidates.

If we regard the fiscal actions in 1960 of President Eisenhower and the Fed as an aberration, then the cycle would have had a span of four years and eight months, close to the normal span for a price cycle. It is reasonable to conclude that President Eisenhower's election-year anti-inflation policy was an exception, since most incumbent politicians are expected to take actions that will assist their re-election or the continuation in office of their political party.

With the exception of the third stock-price cycle, which began in 1957 and ended in 1960, all of the other six cycles began prior to the presidential-election year and ended after the election.

The Biggest Boom and Bust, 1927-32

The severe economic recession of the 1930s had many of its origins in the boom of the 1920s. When the boom finally ended the nation's economy began its descent into the Depression of the 1930s. The pattern of economic boom and bust was to recur many times during the following decades, but not on the scale of the late 1920s and early 1930s.

The boom and bust of the 1920s appear to have had little relation to the presidential election of 1928. The monetary inflation of the late 1920s originated in the easy money policies of the Federal Reserve Board of New York, which was pressured by the Bank of England and other European central banks to inflate the American economy in order to relieve pressure on their currencies. The flood of money released in 1927 and 1928, combined with a mood of unbounded optimism, led directly to the debacle of 1929.

When stock prices began to decline in late 1929, the pyramid of credit on which purchases had been made collapsed, triggering heavy liquidation. Speculators who had bought on margin were forced to sell in order to cover their loans from banks and brokers.

The evaporation of wealth caused by the 1929 stock market crash brought about the economic Depression of the 1930s. In Germany the depression was even more severe than in the United States; one result was the rise to power of Adolph Hitler.

It was during the desperate days of the 1930s that the first steps were taken to control economic ups and downs by means of Federal Government actions. The ability to control the nation's economy opened the way for subsequent abuses, as politicians sought to have a strong economy when it was in their personal interest.

The wild speculation of 1928 and 1929 and the resulting crash were able to occur because the Federal Reserve Board did not have the weapons to slow a skyrocketing stock market. It was several years after the 1929 panic that the Fed was given the authority to set margin requirements.

Easy credit by banks played a large role in the heavy speculation of those years and in the crash that followed. The Fed's easy-money policy of 1927 was a contributing factor in the rapid expansion of bank credit for stock market speculation, which allowed commercial banks to overextend themselves in loans for stock purchases. During the summer of 1927 the discount rate was lowered from 4 percent to 3.5 percent. A year later, in mid-1928, it was raised to 5 percent. In September 1929 the discount rate was raised to 6 percent in New York, but it was lowered to 5 percent on November 1 and to 4.5 percent on November 15, 1929. This was after stock prices had started their steep plunge. But a large percentage of the selling was forced selling because of overextended credit. One estimate has been made that more than a million Americans were carrying about three hundred million shares of stock on margin.

Mass emotion also moved from euphoria—"Be a bull on America" was one slogan of the period—to panic. Inflation quickly changed to deflation and huge losses of values and buying power.

The Roosevelt Recovery and Recession, 1932-38

The depths of the Great Depression were reached in 1932, and in that year the nation's economy slowly began to move upward. Much of the economic recovery was the result of policies taken by the new Roosevelt Administration to stimulate the economy. This was the beginning of the New Deal. By 1936 the nation was well on its way to economic recovery. But it was during this period that the Federal Government gained new controls over the direction of the nation's economy, controls that they quickly learned to abuse.

Federal Government control of the nation's economy and the temptation by American presidents to manipulate the economy for their own purposes started during the New Deal era. In 1936 British economist John Maynard Keynes wrote his *General Theory of Employment Interest and Money,* which advocated government control and regulation of the whole economic life of a nation. The principal instruments of Keynes's policy were to be national budgetary deficits and surpluses, variations in the rate of interest, and the use of government-financed projects. A goal was to manage the economy so that total demand was high, yet not so high as to drive up prices in an inflationary spiral.

Keynes's theories had widespread impact among Franklin Roosevelt's New Deal bureaucrats, and the economist was admired and respected by FOR himself. Many of the policies advocated by Keynes were accepted by Washington and have been used extensively since the Depression years.

This period was the beginning of manipulation of the nation's economy by politicians, frequently for narrow partisan purposes. Franklin D. Roosevelt was probably the first president to take steps following a presidential election to collapse a booming economy deliberately, after having made efforts to create the boom prior to the election. This began the pattern of presidential delight with booming economic conditions prior to the election and publicized presidential concern about inflation following the election.

By 1936 the United States was beginning to recover from the Depression. An editorial in *The Nation* on November 7, 1936, commented: "Whether by good luck or good management President Roosevelt went into the election campaign with economic conditions better, on the whole, than at any time since the end of 1929. This tide of recovery set in so relentlessly in the last few months that the campaign against the New Deal on economic grounds virtually collapsed." The editorial continued: "Even before the recent favorable announcements by the steel companies, the *New York Sun* pointed out that the aggregate net earnings of the first 113 industrial companies had increased nearly 47 percent in the third quarter of 1936 over their earnings in the same period a year ago, while the net profit of the same companies in the first nine months of 1936 was 52 percent higher than in the corresponding months of 1935."*

But the cost of living was also rising. Several months after the election, John Maynard Keynes stated: "The time has passed for the government to try to stimulate business activity and ... it should now devote its efforts to the contrary policy, a deliberate attempt to slow down the forces threatening boom conditions." Keynes's statement was followed by an FOR speech in which he warned that "the dangers of 1929 are again becoming possible, not this week or month but within a year or two," and also blasted the high prices of commodities, particularly copper and steel. His speech reflected his sense that the business of recovery from the Depression was at an end and his new concern with inflation.

The pattern of American presidents waiting until after national elections to signal slowdown policies had begun. A member of the Federal Reserve Board announced that the Government would drop its policy of stimulating heavy industry. The Fed began to tighten credit. Earlier, in August 1936, it had increased member bank reserve requirements by 50 percent.

Stock prices reacted by declining sharply. Another editorial in *The Nation* on May 8, 1937, commented on the reaction: "For a few days toward the end of April it

'Reprinted with the permission of *The Nation*.

seemed as if the scenes of October, 1929, might be re-enacted. Prices had been falling for weeks, from March 6 to April 28 the *New York Times* index of stock prices declined from 142.12 to 126.76, but most of that loss occurred within the last week of the month. What caused the decline? Does it herald a slump in business activity or, as the financial pages of the newspapers tell us, should we dismiss it as a mere reaction from over-speculation? Business conditions in general are extremely satisfactory." The editorial continued: "Since business reports remain excellent, it is evident that we shall have to look elsewhere for the cause of the stock market decline. Two sets of influences appear to be at work, one domestic and the other international. Primary among these is the growing belief that the government intends to check inflation by various restrictive measures. The present recession really started with the announcement of higher reserve requirements for the member banks of the Federal Reserve System. It has received its greatest impetus from the series of warnings which the President has issued against price increases and speculation. These domestic influences have been reinforced by a worldwide drop in commodity prices caused, apparently, by the lessening of the danger of immediate war in Europe.... As matters stand at present, the decline in prices should not be viewed as cause for alarm but as a healthy reaction from over-speculation. Another possibility remains, however. The decline in prices itself might induce a new deflationary cycle. Panic, like boom psychology, is contagious."*

The bear market of 1937 was one of the most severe on record. The Dow Jones industrial average plunged from a high of 195.6 in March 1937 to a low of 98 in March 1938. The nation's economy, which had been starting to boom at the time of the 1936 presidential election, fell into a recession, a newly-coined word. FDR did not want

*Reprinted with the permission of *The Nation*.

43

to be accused of dumping the nation into a depression. But steel production declined to only 19 percent of capacity.

World War II and Immediate Postwar

The threat of war, and then the outbreak of World War II and the great armaments production associated with it, propelled the American economy on to a strong new upward course.

World War II dominated the national economy during the early 1940s, and fear of a postwar recession was the dominant influence during the years immediately following. Wall Street was bearish. The pessimism caused the short interest to reach its highest lqvels since 1933. In November 1948 Harry Truman was re-elected President of the United States with a surprise victory over Thomas E. Dewey. Following the election, stock prices promptly collapsed and continued to decline until mid-1949, when an economic recession that lasted for most of 1949 began.

Cycle 1: 1949-53

The first postwar stock-price cycle began at the June 14, 1949, Dow Jones industrial average low of 160.6. During the spring of 1949 the Federal Reserve decreased margin requirements, thus increasing investors' purchasing power, and three times decreased the reserve requirements of banks that were members of the Federal Reserve System, thus increasing the amount of funds available for loans. In July, President Truman appraised the recession as "moderate" and proposed stimulating the economy.

By 1952 the national economy was booming, aided by the arms produced for the war in Korea. Personal incomes were at record levels and retail spending was at its highest peak ever. In 1952 consumer credit increased by $3 billion to $23 billion at year's end, and home construction had its second-biggest year on record. But there were also warnings of runaway inflation. In December 1952 borrowing by member banks of the Federal Reserve System hit a twenty-one-year high.

From the June 1949 low, stock prices advanced for three years and seven months to a Dow Jones industrial average high of 295.06 on January 5,1953, just two months after the 1952 presidential election in which Republican Dwight D. Eisenhower defeated Democrat Adlai Stevenson.

Within days after taking office, the Eisenhower Administration began making moves to slow down the inflation rate. The Treasury and Federal Reserve Board took steps to trim the expansion of credit. The federal funds rate—the interest banks charge each other on loans—was increased. Efforts were made to cut the budget and to decontrol the U. S. economy. In June the Federal Reserve Board raised the discount rate and sold thirty-year government bonds through its open market operations, thereby taking money out of circulation.

But the nation's economy was already declining into a recession that lasted until the summer of 1954. The hard-money policy was reversed. Credit was expanded; interest rates were kept from going higher; and the Federal Reserve Board lowered the reserve requirements for member banks.

From their January 1953 high, stock prices declined for eight months to a September 15, 1953, low of 254.36, which completed the first postwar stock-price cycle of four years and three months.

Stock-price cycle 1 had a rise of 84 percent (DJI), then a decline of 14 percent.

Cycle 2: 1953-57

The second postwar stock-price cycle began at the September 1953 low. For two years and seven months stock prices advanced to a high in the Dow Jones industrials of 524.4 on April 9, 1956, a presidential-election year. The national economy was again booming. Consumer credit rose sharply. There was an enormous demand for money, which resulted in rising interest rates. Every economic measure indicated that 1956 had eclipsed all previous years; the gross national product rose 6 percent. But the cost of living also increased, and inflation was a problem.

Following his 1956 re-election, in January 1957, President Elsenhower stated in his message to Congress that inflation was the main domestic problem. Several weeks later he threatened to use wage and price controls. One reaction was a severe dip in stock prices. But by July 1957 stock prices rebounded and the Dow Jones industrials rose to within a point of their all-time high reached in April 1956. But in July, Federal Reserve Board chairman William M. Martin stated that "inflation, not deflation, is the real danger." The Fed's tight-money policies slowed the boom. Steel production fell to 70 percent of capacity and automobile output also declined. Inventories were at high levels; the rapid expansion rate of business had created new capacity that had to be absorbed. By the end of 1957 the Fed was moving slowly to make credit more plentiful.

From the July 1957 high, the Dow Jones industrial average declined rapidly to a low of 416.2 on October 22, completing the second postwar stock-price cycle, which lasted four years and one month. The price cycle had a rise of 106 percent, then a decline of 21 percent.

Cycle 3: 1957-60

The third stock-price cycle began at the October 1957 low of 416.2, a level that was almost duplicated again in December, to form a "double bottom" formation on stock charts. In January 1958, during the recession, stock prices began to rise strongly and by year's end were up 37 percent.

The recession was over by early summer 1958 and

the economy again turned strong. By July 1959 employment and personal income were at all-time highs* The U. S. economy was growing rapidly. Housing construction was booming, but housing costs were experiencing upward pressures.

There was a strong bull market in stocks; by July the Dow Jones industrial average had advanced about ninety points since the first of the year. The strength continued for the rest of 1959, finally peaking on January 4,1960, at 688.2 for the Dow Jones industrials.

The booming economy and the continuing rise in commercial loans caused the Fed to become concerned about the increasing demand for money. Businessmen tend to "bunch up" their demand for credit, overspending for capital goods and inventories when business is good. In early September 1959 the Fed increased the discount rate to 4 percent, which was the highest level in twenty-four years, and the fifth increase in the rate since the 1957-58 recession, when the Fed set the discount rate at 1 3/4 percent as an aid to recovery.

The tight-money policies were effective in slowing the economy. Stock prices also declined irregularly for ten months. The Dow Jones industrial average reached its low of 564.2 in October, just a few days before the 1960 presidential election. The October low was the end of the third postwar stock-price cycle.

The declining trend of the economy and the stock market in 1960 was unusual for a presidential election year. Either the cycle timing could not be managed effectively, or 1960 was one presidential year when top policymakers were not trying particularly hard to win the election. It is possible that the 1957-58 recession had occurred too early and that therefore the economy had also rebounded too soon and with too much strength in 1958, thus causing the new cycle to reach its peak too quickly from the point of view of politicians running for office. If restrictive economic policies are started too soon after a presidential election, the deflation-reflation cycle is likely to run ahead of a politically desirable schedule. But it is often necessary to take the step sooner than is desirable if inflation is accelerating at a high rate. From a political point of view a better time to begin slowing the economy is at the end of the first year following a presidential election. This timing would permit about a year to fight inflation with slowdown measures and another year of recovery leading to a highly prosperous period during the next presidential election year, which would be near the top of the cycle. But the desire by presidents to boom the economy prior to elections has also caused them to take anti-inflation measures sooner than would be necessary without the additional stimulus.

During stock-price cycle 3 the rise was 39 percent and the decline 18 percent.

Cycle 4: 1960-62

The fourth cycle in the stock averages began at the October 1960 low, which was 564.2 on the Dow Jones industrial average. Expansive monetary measures were implemented by the Federal Reserve Board during the second half of 1960. The Fed decreased the discount rate twice, decreased margin requirements, and also twice decreased the reserve requirements of member banks. These measures helped to trigger off a strong stock market. Also effective was the rhetoric of presidential candidate John F. Kennedy, who promised to "get the country moving again."

The result was a very strong stock market in 1961. By late 1961 price/earnings levels were the highest in recent history, higher even than 1929. Numerous stocks were selling for forty, fifty, or eighty times their annual earnings. But the mania for growth caused prices to reach levels that discounted earnings too far into the future. Stock prices were too high relative to present and prospective earnings.

Business profits were up sharply in 1961 and the rise was expected to continue through 1962. There was comparatively little inflation in the economy. Although business was improving, there was no boom.

In December 1961 stocks plunged sharply. From the high of 741.3 on November 15, the Dow Jones industrial average declined to 524.6 in April 1962, which completed the fourth stock-price cycle.

Stocks plunged in late 1961 and early 1962 primarily because many investors perceived that prices were too high compared with the price/earnings ratios of stocks in the past. Many large investors were attracted to the yields available from bonds; bond yields had increased their spread considerably over the yields available from stocks. Moreover, beginning on January 1, 1962, the Federal Reserve Board allowed commercial banks to increase their interest rates on savings accounts. Mutual savings banks, and savings and loan associations, also increased their rates. Some investors were probably tempted to take profits and place their capital in a safe place until another attractive buying opportunity came along. One did, only six months later, in June 1962.

The price cycle had a rise of 24 percent on the Dow, then a decline of 29 percent.

Cycle 5: 1962-66

The fifth cycle in the stock averages began at the June 25, 1962, low of 524.6 by the Dow Jones industrials and extended past the 1964 presidential election to 1966. This was a period of buildup for the Vietnam war and the beginning of "Great Society" domestic programs. In November 1963 Lyndon B. Johnson became President of the United States following the assassination of President Kennedy.

In January 1964, a presidential-election year, President Johnson proposed an income tax cut, planned earlier by President Kennedy. The President and his economic advisers predicted that the cut would spark a boom in business that would add $42 billion to the gross national product. The main stimulus for the record boom was expected to be spending by individuals.

The income tax cut became effective in March 1964. The withholding tax rate dropped from 18 to 14 percent, and the amount withheld from paychecks was reduced immediately. Retail sales were up; bank credit expanded; the nation's money supply increased. A deliberately planned boom was accelerating.

But by election day, an election that Lyndon Johnson won by a landslide against Senator Barry Goldwater, concern was being expressed about the increasing inflation. Prices were rising for many raw materials and manufactured items. Wages were also rising. Economist Arthur Burns warned that an inflationary psychology was reasserting itself.

During early 1965 the nation's economy continued to boom. The Federal Reserve Board warned of the deterioration of credit. But by April the crisis in Vietnam had intensified. A bigger war was anticipated. By summer the war in Vietnam had speeded up. The boom in the national economy, which was providing both butter and guns, continued to accelerate.

The stock market rose steadily from its 1962 lows and continued an upward trend through 1963 and 1964. In April and May of 1965 the Dow Jones industrial average dropped about 100 points as a result of the war's intensification. But stock prices rebounded and reached new highs just over 1,000 in January and February 1966. From there they declined steadily for most of 1966, establishing bear market lows on October 10 at 735.7 on the Dow Jones industrial average, which completed the fifth postwar stock-price cycle. The rise was 48 percent (DJI) and the decline 26 percent.

The 1966 bear market was not accompanied by an "official" recession. Nevertheless, the drop

50

in the gross national product was substantial in 1967.

Cycle 6: 1966-70

The sixth postwar stock-price cycle began at the lows set in October 1966; on the Dow Jones industrial average this was 735.7. The price cycle peaked about a month after the 1968 presidential election.

Like most of the economic booms, the boom of 1967-68 was stimulated by heavy Federal Government spending. The fiscal year ending June 30, 1967, had an $8.7 billion deficit and the fiscal year ending June 30, 1968, had a $25.2 billion deficit. This was a period of big spending by Washington for the war in Vietnam and other defense programs, and for welfare, education, and the rebuilding of cities. It was a period of accelerating inflation, and the main culprits were the Federal Government's heavy spending and large deficits, which required it to borrow in competition with individuals and businesses. Commercial banks were forced to rely more on loans from the Federal Reserve. By January 1968 even President Johnson had been persuaded that a tax increase was necessary. In his State of the Union speech he asked Congress to enact a 10 percent tax surcharge for the 1969 fiscal year, which meant that most of the tax would be collected after the November 1968 presidential election.

In February, Federal Reserve Chairman Martin warned of the very dangerous level of speculation in the stock market. He disclosed that the Fed was considering increasing the margin requirement. He blamed speculative excesses on inflation psychology—the belief that inflation would continue and become worse. Stocks declined sharply but quickly rebounded. Credit was gradually tightened by the Federal Reserve Board over a period of several months in order to curb inflation and to strengthen the dollar abroad. The chairman of the Federal Reserve warned again of inflation and blamed the federal budget and its continuing deficits. He predicted that an uncontrollable recession or an uncontrollable inflation would result, and called it the worst financial crisis for the United States since 1931.

By late spring of 1968 rising interest rates and the growing tightness of mortgage credit were hampering home construction, which was also affected by zooming construction costs. Wages set new record highs and retail sales boomed. Economists announced that the inflation spiral could be stopped only by a sizable slump in business activity, but they noted that political pressures weighed heavily against such an inflation cure in an election year. They predicted a recession in 1969.

Meanwhile speculation in stocks was widespread and the volume of trading reached new high levels. The stock market surged on the talk of peace in Vietnam.

By August 1968 the money managers in Washington were being pressured from all sides. The Federal Reserve Board received a vast amount of conflicting advice to tighten or to loosen money and credit. Economists of the Johnson Administration warned the Fed of an embarrassing slowdown in business as early as election day. The cost of credit began to decline. Moves were taken by the Fed to lower the discount rate. High-level officials of the Johnson Administration expressed their delight at the action of the Federal Reserve.

In the fall of 1968 the business boom remained strong. Prices continued to rise. The Johnson Administration revealed that it was not able to make the $8 billion in spending cuts that it had agreed to in the spring in exchange for cooperation from Congress. Chairman Martin of the Federal Reserve Board stated: "We are in the midst of an inflation that is changing the character of this country." He warned of a possible new tightening of money and credit. But the Chase Manhattan Bank in New York announced a reduction in the bank's prime rate from 6.5 to 6 percent. Several days later another banker stated that the Federal Reserve Board had turned prematurely toward a stimulative monetary policy. Other bankers and economists foresaw continued inflation. One pointed out that we have an inflationary bias woven into our system. "When unemployment goes up you get into a politically controversial area," he said.

Several days after the 1968 election, which was won by Richard Nixon over Vice-President Hubert Humphrey and George Wallace, one of Nixon's economic advisers, and the leading authority on business cycles, was interviewed. Dr. Arthur Burns expressed the opinion that expansion in the supply of money and credit should be slowed and that the most pressing problem was bringing inflation under control.

By mid-December there were fears of runaway inflation. Money managers began tightening credit again. On December 17 the Federal Reserve Board ordered the discount rate increased to 5.5 from 5.25 percent. Banks raised their prime rates.

On January 24, 1969, even President Lyndon Johnson, in his final economic report to Congress, called for a strategy that would slowly reduce inflation and the excessive boom in business. He recommended a slowdown in Federal Reserve Board money and credit expansion. The Nixon Administration agreed and the Fed proclaimed its intent to curb credit gradually.

The stock averages began to decline in mid-December and the slide continued irregularly until late May 1970, when the climax of a selling panic occurred. The bottom on the Dow Jones industrial average was at 627.5 on May 26, which was the end of the sixth cycle. The Dow Jones industrial average rose 26 percent, then dropped 37 percent.

A business recession began in late 1969 and lasted for most of 1970. Fiscal year 1969 had a rare budget surplus of $3.2 billion, and fiscal year 1970 had a relatively small budget deficit of $2.8 billion.

The considerable concern and manipulation by top-level officials in Washington lest the national economy might not stay healthy long enough to help their side in the 1968 presidential election once again points up two facts: A strong economy at election time is an important goal to high-level politicians, and they are sometimes inept at attaining that goal. As a result businessmen, employees, stockholders, retirees, and many other Americans all suffer from too much inflationary boom prior to elections and too much economic recession following them. A more stable approach would be to avoid the overstimulus of large-scale federal spending and budget deficits, which would also permit a more gradual approach when tightening money. Equally important would be planning the timing of economic downturns so that they occur later in the political cycle. If a recession occurs too soon after an election, then the recovery is also likely to occur ahead of schedule and might begin a downturn as election day nears. To politicians up for re-election that is bad news, so they are likely to apply pressure for additional economic stimuli, such as tax cuts or increased government spending, even though inflationary pressures would call for the opposite actions.

Cycle 7: 1970-74

The seventh cycle began at the May 1970 trough, which was 627.5 on the Dow Jones industrial average. A change in monetary policy toward more plentiful and cheaper money had been adopted several months before the May trough was reached, and the Fed continued the expansionist policy through 1971 and into 1972. Fiscal policy was also inflationary. The deficit in the federal budget for the fiscal year ending June 30, 1971, was $23 billion, and the deficit for the 1972 fiscal year was $23.2 billion. Following weakness in late 1971 the Dow industrials became strong and trended upward until after the November 1972 presidential election. But inflation was again becoming a large problem, and again a policy of monetary restraint was adopted following the presidential election, which resulted in a gradual slowing down of the economy in 1973 and 1974. Stock prices had their greatest declines since 1929.

The Dow Jones industrial average reached a peak of 1067.2 in January 1973 before starting a long downtrend to the severe sell-off s of 1974. However, other stock averages reached their peaks prior to the Dow industrials. The Dow Jones transportation average reached its peak in April 1972. Standard & Poor's low-priced stock index peaked in the spring of 1971, and the American Stock Exchange market value index reached its peak levels in the spring of 1972. The broadly based New York Stock Exchange composite index, which includes all of the common stocks on that exchange, reached its peak in January 1973, the same month as the Dow Jones industrials. The NYSE average is considered to be the best market average that can be constructed, since it includes all of the common stocks on the New York Stock Exchange, and they are also weighted by capitalization, thus taking into account the variations in size of companies. All of the stock averages completed the seventh cycle during the "double bottom" of October and December 1974. The lowest levels of some stock averages were reached in October; others had their lows in December. The Dow Jones industrial average reached its low in December at 570.0; the New York Stock Exchange composite index and Standard & Poor's 500-stock average had their lowest levels in October.

Stock-price cycle 7 had a rise of 41 percent and a decline of 46 percent.

Cycle 8: 1974-

The eighth stock-price cycle began at the December 1974 low in the Dow Jones industrial average and rose sharply from deeply oversold conditions. A few months later, in April 1975, the nation's economy began to recover from the trough of the recession. The economic stimulus came from federal policies calling for a large decrease in income taxes, a record budget, and expansive monetary policies by the Federal Reserve Board, including decreases in the discount rate and in the reserve requirements of member banks. The results were soaring stock prices and an economic recovery prior to the 1976 presidential election.

Summary of the Stock-Price Cycles

During the last two political-business stock-price cycles, policies fostering economic contraction began soon after each election and stock prices reacted by declining. Following the November 1968 election the bull market high was attained in December 1968, and following the November 1972 election the bull market high was reached in January 1973. But following the 1960 and 1964 elections the bull market continued for slightly more than a year in both cases. The bull market high following the November 1960 election occurred in November 1961, and the bull market high following the November 1964 election came in February 1966. But in both cases, as in the two later cycles, a bear market occurred before the economy began a new rise prior to the next presidential election. The timing of the stock-price cycles is shown in this table.

Table 2

Bear Market Low	Presidential Election	Bull Market High
June 1949	Nov. 1952	Jan. 1953
Sept. 1953	Nov. 1956	Apr. 1956, July 1957
Oct. 1957	Nov. 1960	Nov. 1961
Apr. 1962	Nov. 1964	Feb. 1966
Oct. 1966	Nov. 1968	Dec. 1968
May 1970	Nov. 1972	Jan. 1973
Oct. 1974	Nov. 1976	

The upper turning point of the stock-price cycle following the November 1952 election occurred in January 1953, two months after the election, but the November 1956 election was straddled by a "triple top." Stock prices reached unusual, almost identical, peaks seven months before the election, three months before the election, and eight months after the election. As more investors became aware of the record of stock-price declines following a presidential election there should be a tendency for stocks to reach their highest levels sooner, perhaps even before election day.

Each of the eight cycles has been assisted in its initial price upswing by expansive measures of the Federal Reserve Board. Stimulative monetary policies were taken in 1949, 1953-54, 1957-58, 1960, 1962, 1967, 1970-71, and 1974-75. Each of these periods was close to the bottom of a trough in stock prices. Stock prices rose sharply in each case following the adoption of expansive monetary policy by the Fed.

Chapter 5
Look for Low Risk

One significance of the stock-price cycle to individual investors is that it offers a strategy. Investors should know approximately when to expect opportunities to buy stocks at relatively low risk.

Stock purchases should be made when the risk of loss appears to be minimal and the potential for large gain appears to be very good. In the past the best opportunities for large gains with slight risk have been near the bottoms of the bear markets which have occurred regularly about every four years. The safest time to invest is when the market appears weakest after a long decline. When the national economy is booming and inflation is beginning to be of concern, stock prices often begin to decline because some investors anticipate federal anti-inflation policies such as tight credit. At bear market bottoms, however, this does not appear to be true. Stock prices usually continue to decline in bear markets even after the Fed has switched from a policy of monetary restraint to one of monetary ease. For example, in February and March 1970 there was widespread expectation among economists that the Fed would soon ease up on credit, and the Fed itself stated that tight-credit policies would be relaxed gradually as the year progressed. But it was not until late May that the bear market plunged to its final low and prices began to rebound.

Buy During the Selling Climax

For a general approach to successful investing, plan to purchase stocks when the market is forming a base following a bear market, and plan to sell stock when bull markets are beginning to grow old. Many investors evidently have difficulty taking these actions, particularly when it comes to selling stocks. There is vast professional assistance available in selecting stocks for purchase, but in determining when to sell a stock, the individual investor is usually on his own.

If you are interested in purchasing some stock, and the stock averages are in a bear market, wait until there is evidence which indicates that the end of the downward movement has arrived. The evidence could include very sharp price declines with a big increase in volume, the number of stocks declining vastly exceeding those advancing. If you follow stock prices closely, you will recognize the selling climax when panic selling reaches a peak. Most newspapers will feature the event in banner headlines and stock market analysts will be quoted as saying that the Dow Jones industrials will fall another 150 points. There will be long lists of new lows but few, if any, new highs. If you miss buying during the selling climax, wait a few weeks and you might have a second chance—the market often tests the earlier low, following a technical rally. There will be other evidence that the bear market low is at hand or near. The Federal Reserve Board is likely to begin increasing the nation's money supply. Stock market margin requirements are often reduced. Policies of the Federal Reserve can stimulate the stock market; they can also depress it if the board believes that action is desirable.

During bear markets emotions play a very important role in the sales of securities, particularly when the bear market is in its final selling climax stage. Both sellers and buyers expect lower prices. Sellers dump their stocks in panic because they feel certain that the price will continue to decline. Buyers hold back because they expect even bigger bargains to be available in a few weeks. In this period, when emotions are the dominant influence on stock prices, values become distorted and outstanding buying opportunities are available.

Although most recent bear markets have ended with a selling climax and a strong trend reversal, bear markets do not necessarily have to end that way. Sometimes a bear market bottom can be protracted, and the subsequent bull market recovery slow and gradual.

A more difficult problem arises when you want to invest but the market is not at a depressed, bargain-basement level. However, stock prices move in trends which, once established, tend to continue. It is important to determine whether the trend of the market, as indicated by the various averages, is bullish. The specific stocks that interest you might remain bullish even in a general bear market, but the odds are very good that they will not. In bull markets we usually have a market of stocks, with some very bullish, some bearish, and some inconclusive. But in a strong bear market almost every stock turns weak. Try to determine whether the Federal Reserve Board is tightening or easing credit. Also try to determine the trend of earnings of corporations. The combination of rising earnings and an expanding money supply should indicate a continued bull market.

Trade With the Market's Primary Trend

The most influential factor determining the direction of specific stock prices is the primary trend of the market. So, to be consistently successful in the stock market, it is important to trade with the market's trend. Do not be a bull in a bear market. When there is a bear market, it is wise to be either in cash, ready for a buying opportunity at the bottom of the decline, or a short seller if you are knowledgeable about selecting good candidates for short sales. When the primary trend of the stock market is down, even the best and strongest stocks have difficulty bucking the trend.

When an investor is considering the purchase of securities during periods between the major turning points at bull market tops and bear market bottoms, one of the first things he must determine is the direction of the primary trend. He must also try to estimate how long a major uptrend will continue before a reaction is likely. Normally, the longer an uptrend has been in effect, the greater is the likelihood of a trend reversal. New or young bull markets are safer than stale or old bull markets. This is one reason why daring, aggressive speculators are usually more successful than more conservative investors. They buy earlier, and usually at lower prices, in a new bull market. Investors who wait until they are sure, and they are numerous, are likely to be caught by a reactionary intermediate trend before they have much price appreciation in their stocks.

During years that have experienced bear markets there are many stocks that will remain weak until December and sometimes until the end of the year. This weakness is usually due to continued selling in order to establish losses and sometimes gains for income tax purposes. Since this type of overhanging supply will disappear by December **31,** this time of the year often ranks high for buying opportunities.

In late December 1967, 1 became interested in the California Savings & Loan stocks and purchased shares of United Financial and Wesco Financial. That year had been a bear market year and the S. & L's had been in a decline since about midyear, as shown in Chart 6. As expected, the tax-loss selling ended in late December. I sold the United Financial, for which I had paid $14 in late December, at $24^{3}/4$ the following July, and the Wesco Financial stock, which I had purchased at 15^{7}te on December 11, sold at $28^{3}/a$ in July.

Rebounds are not unusual after the end of selling for tax purposes. In some years the reversal occurs early, around Thanksgiving, as in 1971. That year a buying stampede occurred that was largely technical. Most of the tax-related selling had been completed by then. There were no news developments to change the fundamental nature of the national economy.

Another bear market year was 1966; strong rebounds were experienced by both the Dow Jones industrials and Standard & Poor's Index of 500

62

CHART 6. **UNITED** FINANCIAL CORPORATION OF CALIFORNIA

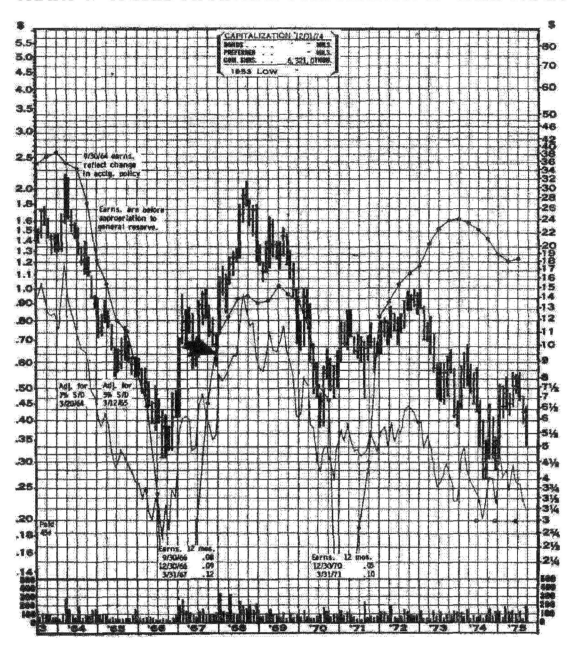

Declining stocks often reverse their downtrends near the end
of the year, as selling for income tax purposes subsides. The
arrow indicates a trend reversal in December 1967.

Chart by Securities Research Company

Composite Stocks. The Dow industrials ended 1966 at about 780. By early February they were at 871. Similar patterns can be found near the end of other bear market years such as 1957, 1960, and 1962. They offer opportunities for alert investors.

In late 1974 the market averages declined to a bear market low on October 4. The market then rebounded strongly and the Dow Jones industrials gained about 100 points. But the market declined again and during the second week in December reached levels slightly above those of October 4. From the early December lows the market advanced mildly. Then, after January 1, prices surged on high volume. The strong market lasted for more than six months. It is interesting to note that the rally occurred while the nation's economy was still sliding into a recession. The strong stock market rally happened because almost everyone who was considering selling would have done so by the end of December, for income tax reasons. With selling for tax purposes out of the way, many investors were aware that the market was seriously oversold and that a rebound was due in spite of the bad economic news. Other buyers anticipated the economic recovery following the recession. So stock market prices moved, as they so often do, months prior to the actual economic recovery.

In late 1975 stock prices again trended downward and again made a low—an intermediatejow—during the first week in October. This was followed by an eighty-point rally and decline, which ended again in early December. From early December the market slowly strengthened and once again exploded in a high volume rally after January 1,1976. The Dow Jones industrial average gained more than 120 points in January, and the volume of trading for the month broke all records on the New York Stock Exchange. Again the removal of the supply of stock being sold for tax purposes was an important cause for the new market strength. Many earnings estimates for the next year are also made in December, an additional stimulus.

Part III
Which Stocks Should You Buy?

Chapter 6
Safety First

The first consideration in buying stock is safety. It is good policy to allot only a fraction of available funds for investment in stocks. It is also important to keep in mind that safety is derived more from the good timing of the purchase and less from the financial strength of the company. The stocks of the nation's largest and strongest corporations have dropped drastically during general stock market declines.

The Biggest Also Decline

When stock market averages reached a new 1973-74 low on October 4, 1974, the two-year decline in the value of stock holdings exceeded $500 billion. The steep decline in market values affected investment companies, mutual funds, pension funds, insurance companies, foundations, and college endowments as well as millions of individual investors. In addition to speculative stocks, the strongest of growth stocks and high-quality stocks of great financial strength were also affected. The drop in market value of IBM exceeded $30 billion, of Sears Roebuck $12 billion, of AT & T $7 billion, and of Exxon $10 billion. General Motors and Eastman Kodak both declined more than $14 billion in value.

The two-year price declines of individual stocks included Avon Products from 140 to $18^5/s$, Polaroid from $143 V_2$ to $14^1/_8$, IBM from $365^1/_4$ to $150 V_2$, and Sears Roebuck from $123\,^1/4$ to $41\,^1/2$. Numerous other quality stocks suffered declines as severe as these.

Price Trends of Income Stocks

The income stocks, most of which are utilities, were in a persistent decline for about a decade because of continued inflation. Compared with the quick, spectacular results that are possible in the well-timed purchase of carefully selected superperformance stocks, those stocks which triple or more in price in two years or less, it is interesting to note what has occurred to income stocks selected because of their large dividends. Chart 7 shows the Dow Jones utility average, which is calculated from the prices of fifteen large electric and gas utility companies. Inflation and the resulting high yields from bonds and high interest rates from bank deposits have had a continuous depressing effect on the prices of most utilities and other common stocks purchased because of their dividends. The only way that income stocks can keep the stock price up is by raising the dividend to a level that is competitive with bond yields and interest from bank deposits. Most other income stocks, including giant American Telephone and Telegraph, shown in Chart 8, also show this downtrend. The plight of the conservative, hold-for-income type of investor was dramatically shown when Consolidated Edison, the big New York City utility, omitted paying its dividend for the first time in eighty-nine years. The stock of the company declined to one-fifth of its 1965 high and the Dow Jones utility average declined to about one-half its all-time high.

The conservative individual investor must learn to buy and sell for his own protection because he has no control over the forces that are responsible for extreme price moves in stocks. Among these forces are the stop-and-go fiscal and monetary policies of the Federal Government, the persistent inflation that continues to erode the value of investment-type securities, the extensive in-and-out large-block speculation of institutional investors, the distortion of earnings by companies, and the extremes of optimism and pessimism

CHART 7. DOW JONES UTILITY AVERAGE

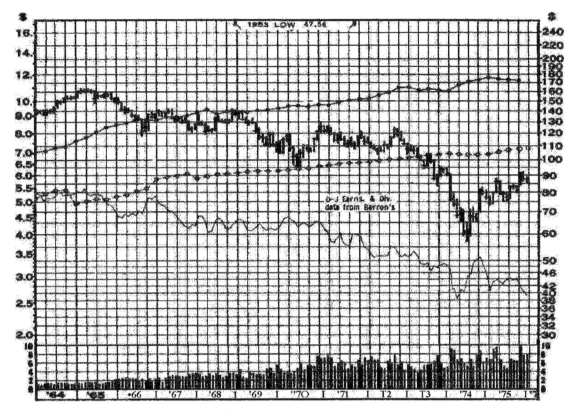

The long-term decline in the price and price/earnings ratios of utility stocks is apparent in this chart. In 1966, 1967 and 1968 the P/E ratio was 15, shown where the earnings line crosses the price bars. Prior to 1966 the P/E ratio was higher, and since 1968 it has been lower. Utility stocks are usually purchased for their dividends.

Chart by Securities Research Company

CHART 8. AMERICAN TELEPHONE AND TELEGRAPH

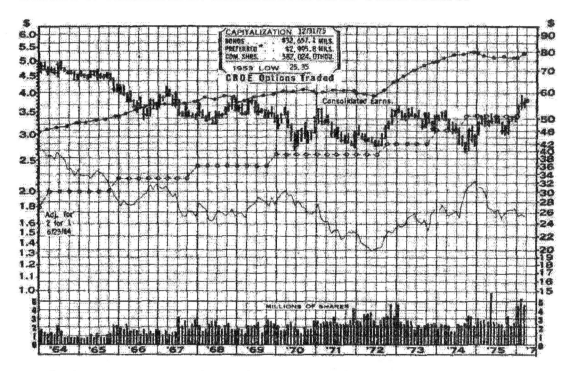

The investment—grade stock of AT & T has had difficulty
regaining its former high price level, which was made in 1964,
although earnings and dividends have increased. In 1964 the
stock had a price/earnings ratio of 25. In late 1974 the P/E
had contracted to 8. AT & T has been a favorite of institutional
buyers for many years. In 1965 shares were owned by 1,066
institutions; 717 institutions held shares in 1976. The price
decline since 1965 of income stocks such as AT & T has paralleled
the long-range decline in bond prices. The company furnishes telephone service to about 82 percent of the country.

Chart by Securities Research Company

found in crowd psychology as unsophisticated investors rush in to buy near the top of bull markets and panic into selling near the bottom of bear markets. There will continue to be booms and recessions, and fears of possible recessions. Cycles of speculation will continue to be with us, offering opportunities to the alert and knowledgeable.

Most Stocks Are Price-Cyclical

For many years certain stocks have been considered to be cyclical; that is, the business of those companies rose and fell with the business cycle. It was also assumed that some industries and certain companies were noncyclical— little affected by the changes in business conditions. The attitude developed among investors that cyclical industries were to be avoided and that others, such as established growth companies, were to be favored. To a certain extent this artificial division of companies into cyclical and noncyclical has been deceptive because although the earnings of some companies might be little affected by the business cycle the price of the stock is often as cyclical as that of companies strongly affected by the business cycle. Virtually all stocks are price-cyclical. Stocks that are not earnings-cyclical often have higher price/earnings ratios, and thus are susceptible to reactions when the primary trend of the market begins to decline. This can occur even during a period of increasing earnings.

The safest time to invest is also the time that offers the best opportunities for large capital gains. To determine the reason that some stocks rise in price, often dramatically, while others decline, I studied over a thousand long-term stock charts, each illustrating twelve years of prices, earnings, and dividends. The review included all of the corporate giants as well as hundreds of small and medium-sized companies. It revealed that the overwhelming majority of price moves during which the price increased to three or more times its original value began as rebounds from the bear market lows of 1962,1966,1970, and 1974. Not only were those periods the safest times to buy, but they also were outstanding buying opportunities for large capital gains. The best time to buy most stocks is when the market looks like a disaster. It is then that the risk is lowest and the potential rewards are highest.

Buy for Large Capital Gains

If you do not seek performance, that is, large increases in value, why buy stocks? When you buy stocks you are taking a substantial risk with your capital. It is much more likely to be partially lost than to be increased. To justify the risk that you are taking, you should expect to be rewarded with big gains. If you do not aspire to big capital gains, you might as well turn your back on the stock market and place your capital in a safer haven, for if you do not use a systematic approach to attain large capital gains, if you approach investing conservatively or use a haphazard method, the chances are good that you will lose much of your invested capital.

I believe that an investor should look for stocks that are capable of tripling in value within two years. Since it is unlikely that the investor will buy the stock at the lowest price and sell it at the highest, it is more likely that he will double his investment rather than triple it. Stocks should not be purchased unless there is a good chance of a big move.

A Superb Company Does Not Necessarily Have a Superb Stock

There is one investment attitude that might be called the "Cadillac Fallacy." Assume that an investor knows that his Cadillac is a good car. He knows that General Motors is a good company. Therefore, he reasons, General Motors is a good stock to buy. A few years ago I listened on my car radio to a stock market analyst being interviewed. During the discussion of the adviser's investment philosophy he stated that investors should buy "quality" stocks.

"What stocks do you recommend?" asked the interviewer.

"Oh, General Motors, AT & T, stocks like that," was the reply.

The twelve-year price histories of these stocks are shown in Charts 8 and 10. They have been in downtrends for years: General Motors since 1965, AT & T since 1964. Keep that in mind when you hear someone say "Buy quality. Stick to the big blue chips." If I had followed that advice in the early 1960s I would not have bought Xerox or Syntex, or Holiday Inns when that company was still an over-the-counter stock.

By November 1974 the price of General Motors stock had declined to a seventeen-year low, "but" some stock experts say, "quality stocks always come back." Possibly so, but you might have to wait a few decades.

Chapter 7
Superperformance Stocks: The Record

The selection of common stocks for large capital gains depends primarily on a search—a search for *Superperformance.* Superperformance stocks are those stocks that make strong, sustained price increases. They are not uncommon; between October 1974 and October 1976 about one stock in every five tripled in price. During the two-year period following the bear market lows in late 1974 there were 243 stocks that I could identify on long-term charts of 1,018 stocks as having tripled or more in price, actions I call Superperformance. I define a Superperformance stock as one that at least tripled in price and increased at a minimum rate of three times during a two-year period. Many stocks had moves that lasted less than two years, and many other stocks had persistent price increases that lasted longer than three years. If the rate of price increase in each case was greater than three times in two years, it is included in the Superperformance category. A move was considered ended if the price failed to reach a new high in less than six months, or if there was a price reaction of 25 percent or more, regardless of the duration of the reaction. There are numerous cases of brief reactions in stocks that were followed quickly by additional strength which multiplied the price many times.

   Superperformance has occurred in well-known growth stocks; it has happened, at one time, in stocks of companies that are now considered to be large, stable, and mature; Superperformance also often occurs in the stocks of companies that are small and little known. It is triggered by many actions, such as a surprise announcement of a large increase in a company's earnings, or the decision of one company to merge with another. *But most often it is found in stocks that are rebounding from oversold conditions, such as those characteristic of bear market bottoms.*

The 243 superperformance stocks that rebounded from the 1974 bear market lows were in addition to 434 stocks that had a total of 589 superperformance moves during the period beginning with the 1962 bear market bottom and ending with 1974 bear market lows. The durations and characteristics of these 589 superperformance moves were studied in greater detail on long-term charts. All are listed in the Appendix.

The analysis of the superperformance moves revealed that 407 of them began as rebounds from the 1962, 1966, and 1970 bear markets; 207 moves began near the bottom of the 1966 bear markets; 44 moves began near the bottom of the 1962 bear market; and 156 began near the bottom of the 1970 bear market. There were 182 superperformance price moves that began at some other time during the period under study.

There were 57 star performers, superperformance phases that experienced price increases greater than 1,000 percent. An additional 162 price moves were greater than 500 percent.

When you invest in common stocks you must make three correct decisions: when to buy, which stocks, and when to sell. The evidence is overwhelming that the really good price gains are made by stocks as they rebound from the lows of four-year cycles.

There has been a wide range in the time span of superperformance phases, from three months to sixty-three, but most of the moves have had durations of eight to thirty-three months. Eleven of the superperformance price moves lasted less than six months; 142 lasted between six and twelve months; 282 lasted twelve to twenty-four months; 124 lasted twenty-four to thirty-six months; and 30 had a duration of more than thirty-six months.

Features of Superperformance Price Action

Superperformance price action is not consistent year after year in even the greatest growth stocks. The stock prices usually move rapidly upward for a period of months or several years. This is the superperformance stage. The superperformance stage might be followed by a price reaction, or a sideways price movement. After a period of consolidation, which sometimes lasts for years, there might be another superperformance stage.

An example of superperformance as it appears on a line chart is shown in Chart 9, which is a twelve-year chart of Skyline Corporation, a major producer of mobile homes and recreational vehicles. The chart shows three superperformance phases. The first superperformance move began near the bottom of the 1962 bear market; the price more than quadrupled in less than a year. The second superperformance phase began at the end of the 1966 bear market; the stock multiplied more than a dozen times in price during the following two years. The third price superperformance phase began at the May 26, 1970 bear market low and ended less than two years later, in early 1972. The price more than quadrupled during that move. Price superperformance phases such as these can be highly rewarding financially in a relatively short period of time, but investors who look for stocks with superperformance potential must know what they are looking for. The search for superperformance candidates must be thorough and systematic, and the timing of the purchase and sale are also vital. But for investors who can make three correct decisions the rewards are often large.

Superperformance and Company Earnings

Many superperformance stock price moves can be correlated with earnings increases by companies. About 38 percent of the superperformance price moves

CHART 9. SKYLINE

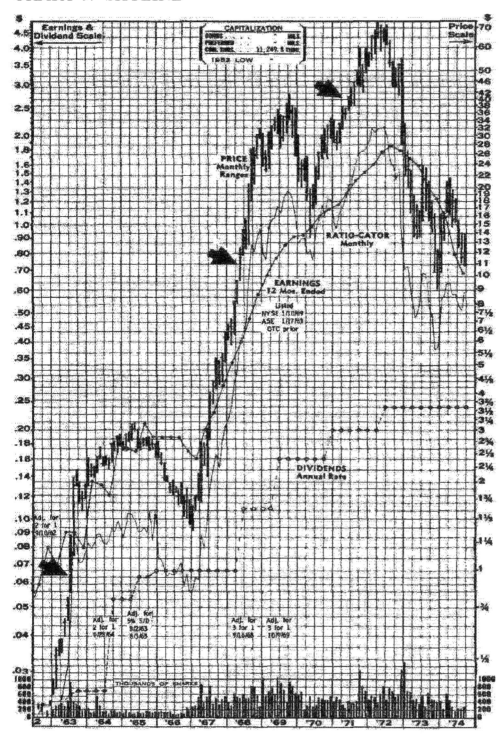

This long-term chart of Skyline clearly shows the stock's three superperformance phases, indicated by arrows. Skyline is a major producer of mobile homes and recreational vehicles.

Chart by Securities Research Company

coincided with or briefly followed large increases in the reported quarterly earnings. In an additional 28 percent a superperformance price move occurred but the earnings were only moderately higher. In about 34 percent of the price moves no correlation could be made between the superperformance move of the stock and earnings gains by the company. In many of the latter group there was a declining trend at the time the price upswing began. Sometimes a trend of increasing earnings began a few months or a year or more after the beginning of the superperformance price move.

A comparison of each stock's price/earnings ratio (the price of the stock divided by its earnings per share) at the beginning of each of the 589 superperformance moves with the price/earnings ratio at the end of each move revealed that the ratio increased in 464 cases. In 69 instances it decreased or remained the same, while in 56 cases there was an earnings deficit at the beginning of the move and P/E computations were not made. Of the 464 superperformance moves during which an expansion or increase in the P/E ratio occurred, there were 86 during which the ratio quadrupled or more. In 118 additional cases the P/E more than tripled, and in another 156 the P/E at least doubled from the beginning of the move to its end. A P/E increase of less than 100 percent occurred during the remaining 104 superperformance moves.

A random sample of 100 of the superperformance moves revealed that 37 percent of the stocks began the move at P/E ratios between 10 and 15. P/E ratios under 10 contributed 33 percent, P/E's between 15 and 20 contributed 20 percent, and 10 percent of the superperformance moves had stocks with P/E ratios above 20 at the beginning of the move.

Superperformance and Company Size

Most strong-performing stocks belong to small companies with relatively few shares of stock. Of the 589 superperformance price moves during the period, in 481 of the moves the company had a capitalization of less than five million shares at the time the price move began. In 58 moves the companies had between five and ten million shares of common stock, and at the beginning of 41 moves there were between ten and twenty million shares outstanding. There were only 9 superperformance moves in the stocks of companies with twenty to thirty million shares, and there were only 2 companies with over thirty million that had this type of price action.

Superperformance and Subsequent Stock-Price Action

Most stocks experience declining prices after a superperformance phase has run its course. A review of the price action following the 589 superperformance moves revealed that in many cases the price decline is severe. Only 85 moves ended without a severe price reaction. The 85 total includes stocks that moved into a sideways price action and stocks that suffered less than a 10 percent retracement of the superperformance move. Of the other 504 moves, within one year 63 began a decline of 100 percent or more of the amount they had advanced that retraced the entire bullish move. An additional 135 superperformance moves were retraced by 100 percent or more declines that began a year or more after the end of the superperformance move. In some cases the decline did not begin until several years had elapsed. An additional 84 moves each had 50 to 100 percent of the bullish move retraced by a decline that began within one year, and 95 bullish moves had 50 to 100 percent of their moves retraced by declines that began more than a year after the bullish superperformance move had ended. Seventy-two moves experienced declines of 10 to 50 percent within one year, and 55 moves were followed by 10 to 50 percent declines that began more than a year after the end of the superperformance phase. Many more superperformance phases have ended in the months of December, January, and April than during the other months, which suggests that income tax factors play a significant role in determining when profits are taken.

There appear to be three principal causes for the price reactions. These include weakness in the stock market in general, including the beginnings of a new bear market; the overpricing of stocks, which often results in profit-taking and a lack of new buying interest; and a drop in a stock's earnings. However, in most of the latter instances the stock's price began its slide before the reported earnings began to decline. In many cases, though, the earnings decline was undoubtedly anticipated by some investors.

Characteristics of Superperformance Stocks

When stocks begin to regain strength after touching bear market lows, which are the stocks that bounce back fastest and strongest? Contrary to a belief held by some investment advisers, it is not the big, quality stocks. The rebounds from the 1966 and 1970 bear market lows were rapid and strong; hundreds of stocks participated. The recovery from the 1962 bear market, however, was slower. Comparatively few stocks rebounded strongly. There were 44 stocks of the 1,018 studied that began superperformance moves that originated at the 1962 bear market lows. They were as follows: ACF Industries, American Airlines, Cerro, Chicago Milwaukee, Chrysler, Columbia Broadcasting, Continental Airlines, Control Data, Culligan International, Delta Airlines, Dennison, Dr. Pepper, Evans Products, General Cable, Greyhound, High Voltage Engineering, Hoover, International Flavors and Fragrances, International Minerals and Chemical, Joy, Massey Ferguson, Motorola, National Airlines, Northwest Airlines, Pan American World Airways, Pasco, Pennzoil, Quaker State Oil Refining, Reading and Bates Offshore Drilling, St. Joe Minerals, Scovill, Skyline,

Syntex, Technicolor, Texas Instruments, Textron, Tidewater Marine Service, Time, Trans World Airlines, United Piece Dye Works, UAL (formerly United Air Lines), UV Industries, Western Airlines, and Xerox.

This list contains the names of numerous companies that later became known as glamour stocks. It has few, if any, stocks that were considered established blue chips in 1962. The budding glamour stocks on the list include nine airlines; air travel at that time was a rapidly expanding industry, and airline stocks also have financial leverage. Many other stocks were of companies with unique new products: Xerox and Dennison (copiers), Syntex (birth control pills), Texas Instruments (transistors), Skyline (mobile homes), and Control Data (computers). Chrysler had just received a new management team.

Rapidly increasing earnings were characteristic of most of the stocks on the list. Another notable feature is their size; these companies were all quite small in 1962. Only one had more than 10,000,000 shares of stock outstanding—Massey Ferguson, with about 13,400,000. Twenty-eight of the forty-four companies had less than 5,000,000 shares of common stock.

This review of the price history of more than a thousand stocks has yielded some good clues regarding the types of stocks we should look for if we want to invest for rapid price appreciation. A winning combination in potential superperformance stock is rapidly rising earnings, a small supply of stock, low P/E ratios, and a product that promises strong future growth.

Chapter 8
Look for Price Volatility

After an investor has concluded that an ideal time has arrived for the purchase of stocks, the next question is: "Which stocks?" To answer that question one of the first features to investigate is price volatility. By reviewing a set of long-term charts an investor can quickly identify those stocks that have had a history of high price volatility and those that have had little volatility. The volatility a stock has experienced in the past tends to continue in the future. It is *a* result of the company's size and the nature of the markets for its products, its financial leverage, and the volume of trading in its stock.

A volatile stock's price rises more in bull markets than the average stock, as represented by the stock indexes, and declines more in bear markets than the average stock. Thus, its price swings are much larger.

The reason for investigating volatility is simply that it is not logical to pick the perfect time to buy stocks, such as near a bear market bottom, and then select a stock that is not likely to rebound strongly because it lacks volatility. Most of the huge, mature corporations, such as the international oils and major utilities, do not have high price volatility; numerous small and medium-sized companies, on the other hand, do.

Large percentage increase in price is caused by a number of factors, but particularly by the size of the floating supply of the stock and the demand for shares by investors. The demand-supply relationship is the main determinant of whether the price is rising or declining, and how fast.

In turn, demand for stock and its availability is determined by several factors including the price level and price action of the stock; the future outlook of the company, including its earnings trend; the trend of and current action of stocks in general; the pessimism or optimism of investors; sponsorship and promotion of the stock; the cost and availability of money; and news developments. Most of these influences should be considered before a specific stock is selected and purchased.

Stock Prices Reflect the Law of Supply and Demand

One of the first subjects covered in a college economics course is commercial competition and the law of supply and demand. Individuals compete in buying and selling services and commodities of all kinds. As buyers, individuals seek to pay as little as possible for the goods, services, or property they want. But they find that others are also in the market for the same things and, as a result, they often have to pay more than they had planned. As sellers, individuals seek to dispose of their goods for the highest possible price, but since many others are trying to do the same thing they often have to settle for less than they had hoped. When the items being bought and sold are popular common stocks, the supply can often be insufficient to meet the demand. The result is an increase in the price of the stock, which brings forth a bigger supply from sellers and reduces the demand of buyers so that a temporary equilibrium is achieved.

The supply is determined primarily by the number of shares in the capitalization of the company. A large company like General Motors, shown in Chart 10, has more than 285 million shares of common stock, while a relatively small company like Jack Eckerd, shown in Chart 11, has only about 17 million shares. Obviously, a strong demand for the shares of Jack Eckerd is going to have a greater effect in increasing the price of the stock than a demand of the same size would have on General Motors.

The big demand is caused by many factors, such as

CHART 10. GENERAL MOTORS

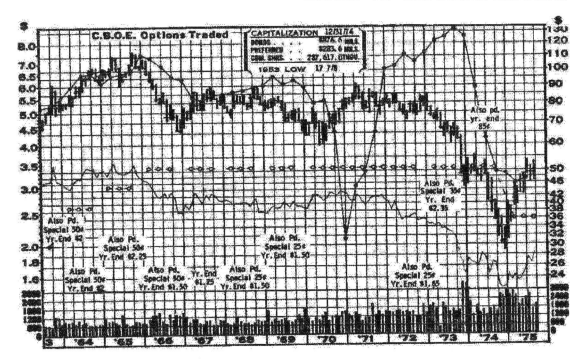

Large companies like GM, which has over 285 million shares
of common stock outstanding, usually have relatively stable
stock prices. But this chart reveals that even high-quality stocks
can be subject to sharp sell-offs. GM declined from about 84 in
early 1973 to 29 in late 1974, a drop of 65 percent.

Chart by Securities Research Company

CHART 11. JACK ECKERD CORP.

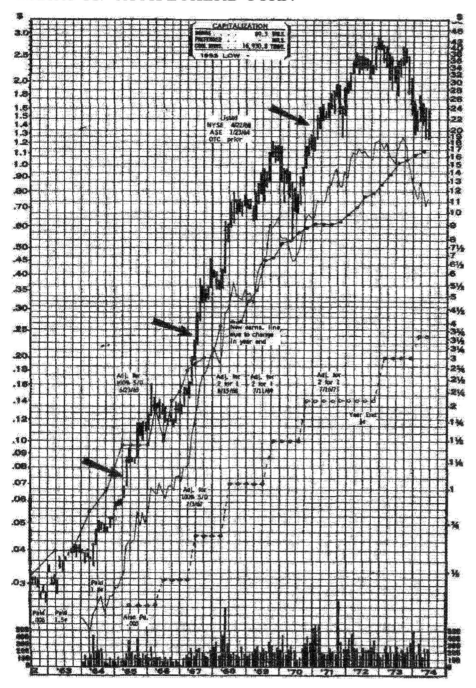

This Florida drugstore chain had fewer than 400,000 shares
of stock outstanding when it began its first superperformance
price move in 1962. In 1966, when the second superperformance
phase started, there were fewer than 800,000 shares. In 1970, at
the beginning of the third move, the company had a capitalization
of about 7,200,000 shares.

Chart by Securities Research Company.

favorable publicity, strong sponsorship, or theavailability of large sums of money for investment. Often it is caused by a new product becoming widely popular. The result can be strong bidding for a relatively small floating supply of stock, creating the classic situation for superperformance price action.

Some of these strongest superperformance price moves have been the result of a severe imbalance between the limited supply of stock offered for sale and the strong demand by investors wanting to purchase the stock. When Syntex was rising in a strong superperformance move in 1963, trading in the stock frequently had to be stopped because of the supply-demand imbalance. After a move in less than twelve months from under 10 to over 190, the move was finally broken by institutions offering large blocks for sale.

Opportunities for big gains in the stock market are more likely to occur in relatively small companies than in companies with many millions of shares outstanding. Look for a small company introducing a unique product that is likely to become widely used. This is the combination that has time after time resulted in dynamic growth and volatile superperformance stock-price action.

The contrast in volatility between low-priced stocks and blue chip stocks can be measured by comparing the performance of Standard & Poor's index of low-priced common stocks with the Dow Jones industrial average, which contains thirty of the largest corporations in the country. Four months after their 1974 bear market low, the index of low-priced common stocks was up 85 percent while the Dow Jones industrial average was up only 35 percent.

A Tale About Volatility and Timing

When I bought KLM Royal Dutch Airlines stock in the mid-1960s at $106\,^3/4$, the stocks of most airlines were doing well. The biggest problem was in selecting the airline stock that would perform best. I chose KLM because of its small capitalization; it had less than a million and a half shares of common stock at that time. In contrast, most of the other airlines then had over six million shares of common. In 1966 KLM was not only a stock with a small capitalization, but the floating supply was even smaller since many of the shares were closely held, 71 percent by the Dutch government. There was a large and growing short interest. The result was great volatility. By watching a stock of this type closely, on a daily basis, it is almost possible to predict its volatile moves. When the price jumped, heavy short selling would soon follow. Any price weakness would bring in short covering, driving the price up again.

The monthly short-interest figures are summarized and published in the *Wall Street Journal* and other newspapers about the twentieth of each month. Many short sellers would cover their short positions prior to the publication of the statistics because they were afraid that an increase in the published figures would cause the stock to jump again, jeopardizing their short positions.

I finally decided to sell my KLM stock because its chart showed an unsustainable spear pattern, a near-vertical formation, which often means heavy profit-taking and a price reaction. I decided to sell at about ten thirty on the morning the short interest was published because I assumed that panicky short covering would run up the price of the stock on the day prior to the publication of the statistics and that a certain amount of this action would also occur shortly after the figures were released. I called my broker and told him that I wanted to sell all of my KLM that morning because I expected it to be the final top in the stock. I asked him how the stock was doing. "It's up about four points," he said.

"Well," I replied, "if it is still going up there is no point in my selling now. I had expected it to top out this morning. Will you keep an eye on it and call me right away if it starts to drop?"

He replied that he would. By eleven o'clock I had received no phone call. I was beginning to become apprehensive because I was absolutely certain, having watched the price action of the stock for a few months, that it would reach the final peak that morning. I called my broker again. "How is KLM doing now?" I asked.

"Down four points," he replied.

"Sell it. Sell all of it." I told him.

That summer morning in 1966 was close to the final top for KLM. From a price of $155\,{}^3/4$ in 1966, KLM eventually declined to $13\,{}^1/4$ in 1974. This is another illustration that price superperformance moves in phases. The individual investor must be able to identify stocks early in their superperformance phase and sell when there is evidence that superperformance is approaching its end. When there is new evidence that the fundamentals of a stock, such as earning power, are weaker than previously estimated, the strong demand for the stock also disappears.

Price Distortions by Stock Exchange Specialists

The normal supply-demand relationship is severely distorted by the primitive specialist system still permitted to operate at the stock exchanges. The specialists are stock exchange members who buy and sell on the floor of the exchanges and who are assigned by the stock exchange to make a market in specific stocks. In actual practice they are often the antagonists of the public investors.

When stocks are rallying and the public is buying, the specialists are usually sellers and short sellers. Short selling is the selling of stock not owned by the seller. It is accomplished by borrowing stock. The short seller expects a price decline which would allow him to buy an equal number of shares at a lower price, permitting him to return them to the lender and to make a profit from the difference between selling and covering prices.

Heavy short selling by specialists gives them a vested interest in having the stock's price decline to a lower level, so that they can cover their short sales and make a profit. The price decline is forced by heavy short selling at the top of the rally. The forced price decline cools buying pressures which might otherwise continue.

In spite of heavy short selling, which drives down stock prices, over a longer period of time the normal buying and selling pressures should be more influential. Short sellers must eventually buy back or "cover" their short sales.

Specialists have developed into a fine art their techniques for driving stock prices down. Theoretically they are supposed to be responsible for maintaining an "orderly market" by minimizing wide fluctuations in their assigned stocks by purchasing and selling for their own accounts. But their motivation to support prices often does not appear to be as strong as their desire to depress prices. During the spring of 1976 I happened to observe a stock listed on a regional stock exchange that had fallen $3^1/4$ points, or about 19 percent in a single trading session, from $17^1/4$ to 14. The volume of trading was only six hundred shares, so the specialist did not appear to be supporting the price, which rebounded the following day.

On another occasion I noted a news item that appeared in a financial publication with the headline "Stock Exchange Fines, Censures Specialist." The news story described how an individual in a specialist firm allegedly failed to make an orderly market in a stock. He was charged by the exchange with opening the stock at too low a price, thereby triggering the sale of investors' stop orders, which were executed when the stock's price declined to specific levels. The opening price was the low for the day. It caused stop orders for a substantial number of shares to be executed. These examples illustrate the hazards investors might face from the activities of stock exchange specialists.

Look for Rebounds

The strongest rebounds usually occur when the entire stock market is drastically oversold, as in 1962, 1966, 1970, and 1974. When the recovery begins, hundreds of stocks take part in the strong recovery action. Some manage within months to regain the price level that they possessed prior to the sell-off. Other stocks might not ever regain their former levels. The challenge to the investor is in attempting to identify the stocks that will rebound the fastest and the highest.

On October 4,1974, stock market averages reached new lows in a bear market that had started in January 1973 for the Dow Jones industrials, and in December 1972 for more broadly based averages. The Dow Jones industrials declined from a January 11,1973, high of 1067.2 to a Decembers, 1973, energy-crisis low of 783.56. Following a rally in March 1974 to 878.13, the stock average began its long decline to the October 4 low near 573. The last stage of the decline included a precipitous drop of more than 200 points between August 7 and October 4, a Friday. On Monday, October 7, the market staged a strong rally; the Dow Jones industrials advanced 23 points. Following a 4.93 drop on Tuesday, the averages advanced an additional 55.54 points during the next three days to finish the week at 658.17. This was a typical "buyer's stampede" caused by large numbers of investors attempting to buy the bargains created by the severely oversold condition of the market. On the following Monday, October 14, the strong advance continued. During the six trading days the Dow Jones industrials had advanced more than 100 points. This type of strong rebound is typical of price movements at the bottom of bear markets. It indicates a major price reversal and is the best time to make purchases.

Which Stocks Rebound?

The big question we have been asking is: "Which stocks?" By studying stock tables closely during this period you can determine which stocks are rebounding strongly and which are not responding. Many of the strong rebounders are likely to become the market leaders. For that reason it is important to identify those stocks and their characteristics.

After reviewing the monthly Security Charts of 1,105 leading stocks published by the Securities Research Company, I was able to determine quickly the stocks with the largest percentage increases during the October 4-11 rally. There were seventy-nine stocks that increased by at least 35 percent during the six-day period. Although it is not likely that all of the seventy-nine stocks would continue to be so strong that they would increase by 300 percent over a two-year period and thus become superperformance stocks, it is very likely that many potential superperformance stocks are included in the list. The strong-rebound stocks are likely to include many of the new market leaders for the next two years.

Stocks that rebounded the most from the October 4, 1974, market low included oversold stocks that had been declining sharply prior to the rebound. Most were companies with strong fundamentals, including rising earnings trends. Small capitalizations were more numerous than companies with large capitalizations; the large, mature, primary blue chips were not represented.

Of the seventy-nine stocks, forty-two had capitalizations of fewer than ten million shares, and of these twenty-three had fewer than five million shares. Nineteen stocks had between ten and twenty million shares, seven had twenty to thirty million shares, and eleven had more than thirty million shares. The largest capitalization was seventy-eight million shares.

Four airlines were among the strong rebounders, but the largest group was the drug companies; ten of them had price increases of over 35 percent. Drug stocks were not the strongest group, however. There were three groups of stocks that reached their lows two to four weeks prior to the October 4 lows recorded by the market averages and the vast majority of stocks. These three groups of stocks included the offshore oil drilling companies, which "bottomed" during the third week in September and subsequently rallied stronger than any other group; the mobile home stocks, which also began to rally then; and the savings and loan stocks, which turned strong early in September. These three stock groups led the rebound in prices. The mobile home and savings and loan stocks were rebounding from severely depressed conditions in those businesses, and prospects for improvement seemed bright because the Federal Reserve Board had adopted policies for easier money. The offshore oil drilling and drug industries had not been depressed but these stocks had declined because of the general bear market for stocks.

In contrast to the strength shown by these groups and many other stocks, some large, mature companies continued to decline to new lows during the strong upswing in the market averages. The savings and loan, offshore drilling, and mobile home stocks, which were the most prominent leaders in the advance, are volatile, speculative stocks, not blue chips. Most have small capitalizations. Some of the offshore drilling stocks doubled in price during that brief period.

A large short interest, which is the number of shares that have not been covered or repurchased, combined with a small capitalization, can often cause a stock to jump in price when the market turns bullish. Fifteen of the seventy-nine stocks had short positions of at least twenty thousand shares when the strong rally began.

This review of strong rebounders from the October 4, 1974, low does not include all strong stocks, of course, since there were a few stocks which declined very little or not at all during the plunge that included most stocks as well as the averages. Although they did not decline during the strong sell-off that affected most stocks, neither did they rally as strongly during the rebound phase.

It appears that many stocks that are relatively strong during a bear market are in their own up-cycle, with increasing earnings and sales, and a future that appears bright. But the stock's price trend is dominated by the bearish primary trend of the general market, which causes the price to decline along with most other stock prices, but not as severely. When the bearish market turns bullish, stocks that are in their own earnings up-cycle should also turn bullish. This is not true of stocks that are in their own bearish cycles, however; even after the primary market trend turns bullish they are likely to remain relatively weak because of their own down-cycle of declining or static earnings and sales, or an unfavorable company outlook.

Emotional Selling and Trend Following

There are many occasions when strong stocks are battered down to bargain-price levels by the highly emotional selling typical of a bear market. Chart 12 shows the price and earnings record of Natomas, a shipping company that also holds extensive petroleum interests in the Java Sea and off Sumatra. In 1969 the price reached a high of 130, then descended to a 1970 bear market low of 13, but rebounded to 101 in 1971. Euphoria about a relatively small company discovering new oil resources caused the price to zoom up; heavy short selling followed by panic selling caused the decline. The rebound occurred as short sellers purchased stock to cover their sales. Trend followers saw the stock's price rising sharply, so they also started buying. News items also played a part.

Natomas is an unusually volatile stock, but the same situation can be found in regard to many other

CHART 12. NATOMAS

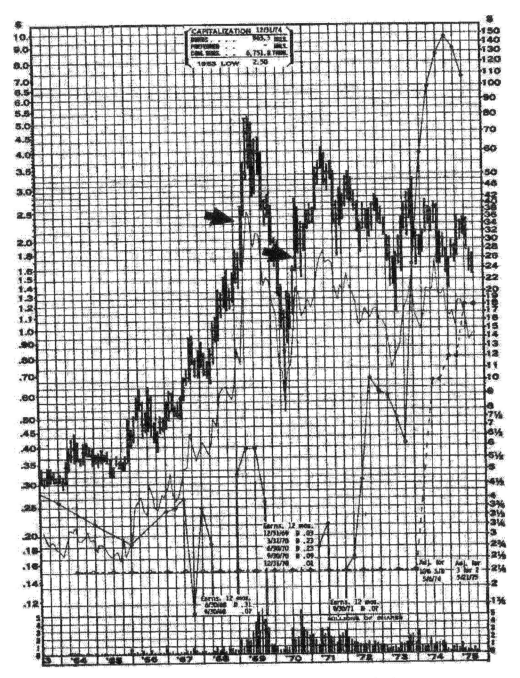

One of the strongest rebounds from the 1970 bear market
bottom was made by Natomas, which had a large short interest,
a small capitalization, and considerable publicity and sponsorship. With large oil reserves in Indonesia, investors were anticipating a bright future for the company. Superperformance
moves are indicated by arrows.

Chart by Securities Research Company

stocks: heavy emotional selling during bear markets in stocks that rebound strongly. General market declines such as those of 1962 and 1970 create opportunities to pick up excellent stocks at bargain prices. Many stocks decline not from any inherent weakness but because they were driven down by heavy short selling followed by panic selling.

When the market is close to a selling climax after a long decline, the stocks that are likely to rebound the fastest are often active stocks with strong fundamentals and small capitalizations that have been sold heavily in the general market decline.

Leverage

Financial leverage in a stock is often responsible for high volatility in the stock's price because the company's reported earnings can fluctuate greatly if there are large amounts of debt in the capitalization.

Stocks with leverage often present opportunities for profit, but the timing of the purchase and the sale must be good, for a stock with high leverage can be risky. A stock has high leverage if the company has a large proportion of bonds and preferred stock relative to the common. If a company has bonds outstanding for several million dollars, the bond interest will be deducted from income and the remainder will be left for the common stock. Assuming that a company has income of $500,000 but $400,000 must go for bond interest, there is $100,000 left for the common stock. But a relatively modest increase in income to $600,000 the next year results in a doubling of the amount for the common stock, from $100,000 to $200,000.

Perhaps the most familiar use of leverage is in real estate. If a home buyer purchases a $50,000 house and obtains a $40,000 mortgage on it, he is actually investing only $10,000 of his own capital. If the house rises 20 percent in value and is sold for $60,000, a profit

96

of $10,000, or 100 percent will be realized on the investment of $10,000. On the other hand, if the house drops in value by only 20 percent, and the buyer sells it for $40,000, he would lose 100 percent of his investment of $10,000.

Leverage is common in the capital structure of many industries, such as airlines and utilities. In a utility, bonds and preferred stock may account for two-thirds of the invested capital, with the common stock representing the balance. The result is that the common shareholder enjoys a high degree of leverage. Fixed charges, the payment of interest on the bonds and dividends on the preferred stock, must be made before the common stock is entitled to receive any. But once the fixed charges are paid, the balance goes to common stock. Thus, as total income rises, common share earnings begin to show a larger percentage gain than total profits. When earnings decline, the percentage drop in the common share profits is larger than the percentage decline in total income. This is the great danger in high-leverage stocks.

Most utilities have a fairly consistent income, but when high leverage is combined in a company with an erratic income pattern—such as certain railroads or companies strongly affected by the business cycle-volatility in the earnings per share can occur, which is often reflected in even greater volatility in the price of the stock. The earnings record and price performance for Trans World Airlines is shown in Chart 13. The company has $958 million of bonds in its capitalization and also preferred stock, therefore high financial leverage.

Financial leverage is also a characteristic found in stock warrants, stock options, and in many low-priced stocks, particularly in cases where the stock has formerly sold at much higher prices and where each share of common stock has considerable potential earning power behind it. In situations where there is a high volume of dollar sales relative to shares of common stock there is operating leverage. Retail stores, such as grocery chains, often have a high volume of sales but

CHART 13. TRANS WORLD AIRLINES

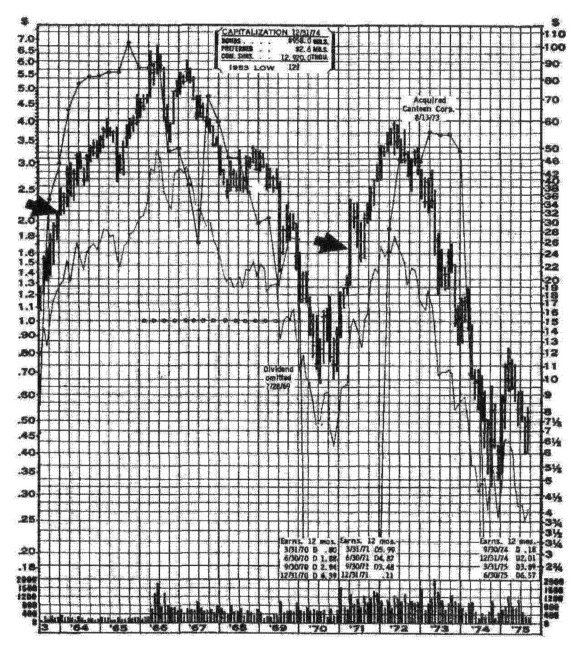

This airline's history of price volatility is apparent on its
twelve-year chart. A comparison of the price ranges with the
earnings line, which is also on the chart, reveals that earnings
peaked before the price in 1965-66, but the price reached a
peak prior to the earnings in 1972-73. Severe price declines
from 1967-1970 and from 1972-1974 paralleled declines in
earnings.

Chart by Securities Research Company

relatively narrow profit margins. Any improvement or deterioration in margins has a strong impact on the earnings per share of common stock.

High leverage is also involved when the discovery of a large new oil field or metal ore body is made by a small company. If the discovery is made by a large company the leverage is much smaller, since the increase in the value of assets per share would be less. Margin accounts, which use borrowed money to purchase securities, are another well-known example of the principle of leverage.

The Dangers in Leverage

Safety is sacrificed when you select a stock with high leverage in preference to one with small leverage. A company with a very large debt burden is in greater danger of going bankrupt, as in the case of the Penn Central. For that reason financially conservative companies are preferred by many investment advisers. However, financial strength did not prevent the value of General Motors stock from declining in 1974 to less than one-third of its 1965 price. Financial strength did not prevent IBM from declining in less than two years from $365^1/4$ to $150^1/2$. Nor did financial strength prevent debt-free Polaroid from falling from $143^1/2$ to $14^5/s$. But leverage and the financial strength of companies should be thoroughly studied and evaluated before stocks are selected for purchase. When money is tight and expensive, companies with large cash positions are at an advantage, particulary if they know how to use their financial resources effectively.

The October 12, 1974, *Business Week* had a very useful tabulation showing the debt of companies as a percent of equity. By studying this information an investor can quickly determine which companies have highly leveraged debt structures and which do not. The debt of Eastman Kodak, for example was 5 percent of equity. For General Motors it was 10 percent; for Lockheed 308 percent; for Trans World Airlines, 249 percent; and for McCrory, 799 percent.

During periods of recession, when profits decline for most businesses, companies that have large amounts of debt sometimes have no profits at all. But as the national economy emerges from recession, corporate sales and profit margins begin to increase. The percentage increase in profits can usually be much larger for stocks with large leverage than for stocks with small leverage. Highly leveraged companies, then, are even more business-cycle-sensitive, and often are buying opportunities when the stock's price is depressed.

Leverage in Low-Priced Stocks

Another type of leverage is that found in low-priced stocks and warrants.

Of the 152 superperformance moves that began at or within six months of the 1970 bear market lows, 107 started from a price below twenty dollars. Only five of the superperformance stocks began their rapid rises at prices above fifty dollars. Fourteen began at prices between thirty and fifty dollars; twenty-one of the stocks started between twenty and thirty dollars. The largest number of superperformance moves, 71, began at prices between ten and twenty dollars. There were 33 moves that began at prices between five and ten dollars, and three that began at less than five dollars a share.

This tabulation indicates that the best place to look for potential superperformance stocks is among common stocks that are selling in the five- to twenty-dollar range. Comparatively few high-priced stocks move into superperformance price action.

Companies that are strongly affected by the business cycle, such as those in the construction industry, often have abrupt declines in sales and earnings that are only temporary. Stock prices react to these business declines, however, and sometimes present investors with outstanding buying opportunities. When the business cycle shows evidence of turning up, many cyclical stocks also pick up strength. Many low-priced stocks have low prices only temporarily, and are capable of regaining much higher price levels when the business climate improves. The important feature to look for is strength. Determine if the company has the resources to rebound and to bring its stock back to its former high esteem. Quite often earnings are only temporarily depressed and will improve. Other factors, such as announced expansions or new products, will sometimes give new life to a depressed low-priced security.

One of the quickest ways to identify low-priced stocks that might have the potential to regain former high price levels is to review a set of long-term charts. An example of this type of situation is shown in Chart 14 of Holiday Inns. After finding candidate stocks by reviewing charts, evaluate the stock and company thoroughly prior to making a purchase.

Leverage in Warrants

A warrant is an option issued by a company that gives its owner the right to purchase a specific number of shares of the company's common stock at a specific price and prior to a specific date. There are a few warrants granting a perpetual right to buy stock. Warrants have become numerous in recent years, numbering in the hundreds. They are generally issued in association with financing programs, making bonds or preferred stock more salable. The warrant is detached and is traded separately.

Warrants are highly leveraged; they can rise much faster in terms of percentages than the common stock, and can decline much more rapidly. The value of warrants is also determined by the amount of time remaining before the expiration date, since they become

CHART 14. HOLIDAY INNS

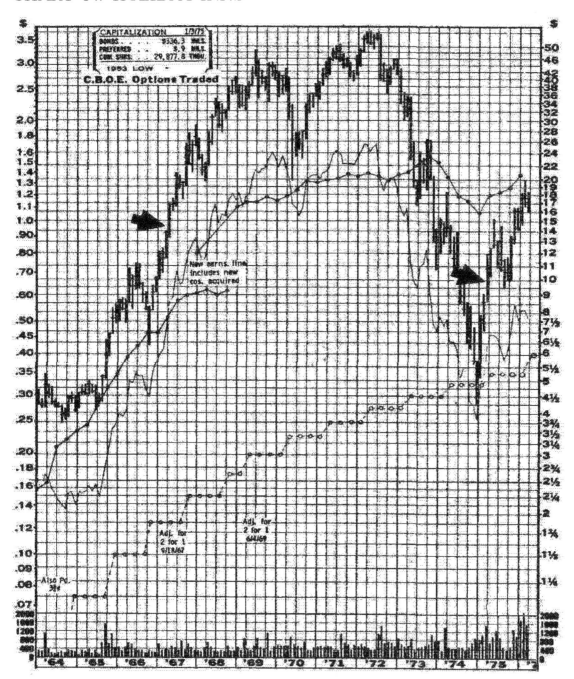

Holiday Inns has a network of over 1,500 motels in all states, Canada, and overseas. The stock's price began declining even prior to the oil crisis of late 1973-early 1974, but it also rebounded strongly from its 1974 bear market lows.

Chart by Securities Research Company

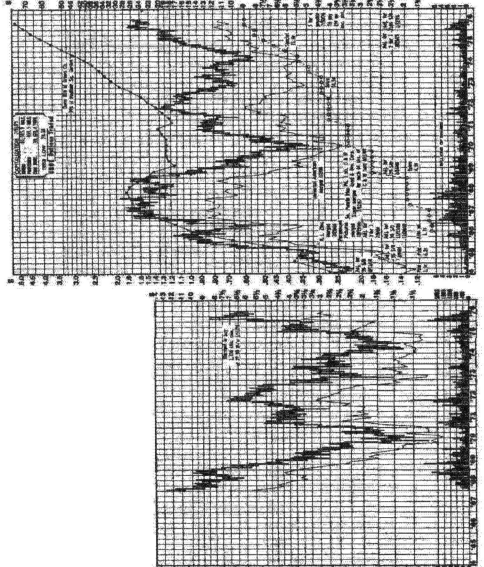

The volatility often characteristic of warrants is shown in this chart. Warrants have greater leverage than the common stock when the common stock is selling below the exercise price of the warrant. Since most warrants have expiration dates, the safest are those warrants that have several years before expiration.

Chart by Securities Research Company.

worthless after that. When a stock is discovered that appears to be capable of a superperformance move, always check to see if there is also a warrant.

The most important factor in selecting a warrant is the price movement of the common stock on which the warrant is based. If the common stock appears to be a good investment, a warrant based on the stock is likely to be an even better performer. Chart 15 shows the relative performance of the warrants and common stock of Gulf & Western. The stock increased in price from about 8 !/2 in late 1974 to 26 in early 1976. During the same period the warrant increased from 1 V2 to $8^{1}/2$. During declines the warrant lost much more value than the common stock. Between early 1972 and late 1974 the warrant declined from 7 to 1 $^{1}/2$ while the stock dropped from 20 to $8^{1}/a$. Leverage is a more important factor when the common stock is selling below the exercise price for the warrant; above the exercise price the stock and warrants move together, point for point.

In addition to the leverage, the other big advantage of the warrant is that less money is required for the same action. But it is always important to keep in mind that there is an expiration date. Avoid warrants or stock options that have less than a year to go before the rights expire and the options become worthless. Requiring an investment to perform within a short period of time severely limits the possibilities of success.

104

Chapter 9
Look for New Earning Power

The primary objective of companies is profit, which is then used to finance further expansion of the company or is paid out to stockholders in the form of dividends.

Companies are not in business to make automobiles or soap or television sets or widgets. The reason for their existence—the reason that entrepreneurs invest capital, imagination, and energy—is to make money. If there were no profit motive there would be no reason for enterprising individuals to go to the effort of organizing and building up businesses. Since profit, or earnings, is the reason for the existence of companies, investors should evaluate companies from the point of view of their profit-generating potential.

In most well-established companies earnings can be quite accurately forecast from year to year if there have been no extensive changes in the business. To a large degree the forecasting is simply a matter of projecting trends. In these cases stock prices usually reflect the profit situation as it exists and as it is expected to continue. Most large companies are little affected by changes such as new products. Their product lines are so extensive that one or two variations make little difference.

But there are numerous smaller companies that are strongly affected by change, and their stock prices sometimes do not reflect the changes that are taking place—changes such as the development of a new product or a shift in management. One place to look for new earning power is where change is occurring.

Change and Stock Prices

Change means opportunity, and change is one thing that is certain. Wars begin and wars end eventually. Federal monetary policy causes tight money, then policies change and money becomes plentiful. New presidents are elected and the old retires from the scene. Technology creates new products for the consumer. Companies are organized, grow, mature, and decline. Many grow very little or not at all before they disappear from the scene. But through the entire panorama there is change.

Technological change during the past century has afforded investors countless opportunities for profit. A hundred years ago there was railroad building. Then the automobile was developed; then the airplane; and electricity; and radio. During the past two decades fabulous growth has occurred in areas encompassing computers, copying, color television, rocketry, electronics, birth control pills, mobile homes, and travel. Well-managed and innovative companies in these fields, and many others, have had outstanding growth. Many stockholders who purchased shares of these companies in their early stages have profited handsomely. Today there are other companies in a similar early stage of development. Finding them requires that the prospective investor conduct a search that must be systematic in order to avoid overlooking a possible winner.

Change taking place in a company might also involve a change in management or the acquisition of another company. It might involve a major mineral or oil field discovery. But change implies the introduction of a new element that has not been taken into account in the previous evaluation of the company's worth. Thus a re-evaluation occurs, moving the price of a share up or down in value.

The introduction of new competitive products is a change that can often be particularly significant. For example, what will be the significance to Xerox of IBM's entry into the copier market? What will be the significance to Polaroid of Eastman Kodak's competitive instant photography? What is the long-range meaning for Detroit of the sales entry of Japanese automobiles into the U.S.?

Change Resulting from Discoveries of Natural Resources

Dramatic change occurs and superperformance price action takes place when a natural resources company makes a big oil field discovery or a mining company discovers a big new ore deposit. Large strikes dramatically increase the assets and earning power of a company, particularly if it is relatively small. For example, the announcement in April 1964 by Texas Gulf Sulphur that it had discovered a major body of copper, silver, and zinc ore in Canada resulted in strong superperformance price action in its stock. Purchasers should keep in mind that it is important to buy early in situations of this type. The most dynamic part of the action often occurs in a matter of days, or even hours. Sometimes in the stock market he who waits too long is likely to be the loser.

One place where change has occurred in recent years has been in the offshore oil and gas drilling business. The consensus of opinion among drilling contractors has been that prosperity for the industry would last at least a decade. Moreover, in order to meet the anticipated demand for petroleum, the American Petroleum Institute has estimated that world offshore oil output would have to quadruple by 1982.

The price and earnings record of one of the independent companies in the industry, Vetco Offshore Industries, is shown in Chart 16.

Change in Government Policies

Changes in government policies have a wide-ranging influence on stock prices. For example, the Federal Reserve Board frequently changes the amount of cash required by the customer to purchase stocks on margin. Since 1950 there have been five periods during which the margin requirement was set at 50 percent. That is, the customer needed only half of the money required

CHART 16. VETCO OFFSHORE INDUSTRIES

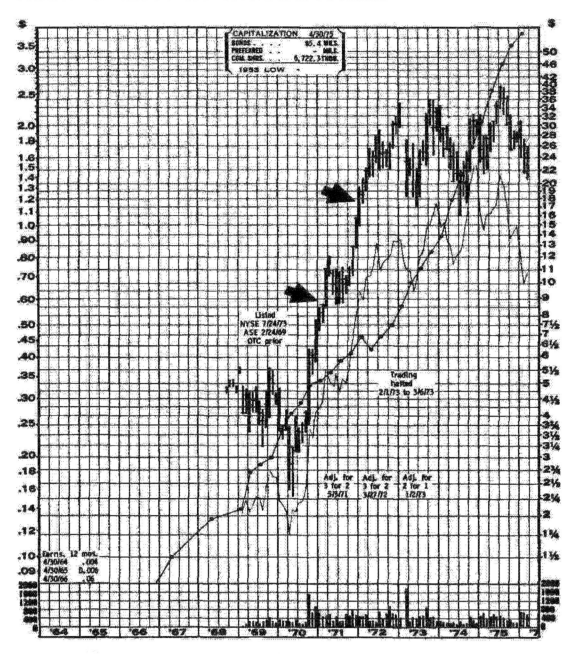

This company is one of the group that is benefiting from the continuing boom in offshore drilling operations for oil and gas. A new manufacturing facility for offshore equipment was completed in 1974. The earnings have been increasing steadily and are expected to continue. Superperformance is indicated by the arrows.

Chart by Securities Research Company

for the stock purchase; the other 50 percent was borrowed from a bank by his broker. At other times since 1950 the margin requirement has been at 55, 60, 70, 75, 80, and 90 percent. A high margin requirement obviously curtails the amount of buying on credit that can be done. It is normally used when the market is very bullish; a lower margin requirement is set when the market is depressed. Lowering the margin requirement has the effect of adding billions of dollars of potential buying power that can be used for the purchase of stocks.

Changes in the capital gains tax are under consideration in Congress. It has been estimated that about $20 billion in securities are frozen because their holders are reluctant to sell and be liable for the tax. Some congressmen would like to make changes in the law that would lower the capital gains tax rate.

Some government policy changes, such as increased expenditures for highway construction or military hardware or medical research and equipment, offer many opportunities for alert investors. Other changes, such as modifications in import restrictions, might spell potential trouble in the future for some companies. Awareness of new inventions, new policies, and developing world events is essential for successful investment.

Technological Change

The introduction or planned introduction of a unique new product can have a dynamic effect on the price of the stock of a relatively small company. Many investors tend to be attracted to new, developing situations and to ignore old, established, stable situations. A large, mature company is likely to remain relatively stable in price, thus offering comparatively little opportunity for large capital gains.

Bausch and Lomb, although a relatively small

company, has been an established manufacturer of optical products for many years, producing eyeglass lenses and frames, and scientific instruments. Several years ago the company announced that it had acquired the rights to produce a revolutionary new "SOFLENS" contact lens. The announcement was given a considerable amount of publicity on financial pages. When the information was released in early 1971 the volume of trading in the stock increased tremendously, as can be determined from the vertical bars at the bottom of Chart 17. The price of the stock also made a very large jump, quadrupling within a few months.

Similarly, in early 1972, numerous investors suddenly developed Wankel fever as the new rotary engine was publicized. The stock of Curtiss-Wright, which holds the North American license for the Wankel-type rotary combustion engine, jumped more than 500 percent on high volume in less than seven months as news stories described interest in the engine by the major automobile manufacturers. Eventually, as interest in the new engine diminished, the price of the stock declined to its pre-Wankel level.

These two cases illustrate the reaction that investors sometimes have to the introduction of a unique new product by a small company. Most newly developed products are not as highly publicized as these, but often the new product, sometimes after a number of years, does add substantially to the company's earnings. Widely sold new products can also give sizable boosts to the sales and earnings of large companies, as the development and sale of the Instamatic camera did for Eastman Kodak. But the effect on the price of the stock of a large company is not as dramatic.

Growth-Stage Companies

Many new companies are born every year; some will not survive. Others reach their rapid-growth stage and

CHART 17. BAUSCH AND LOME

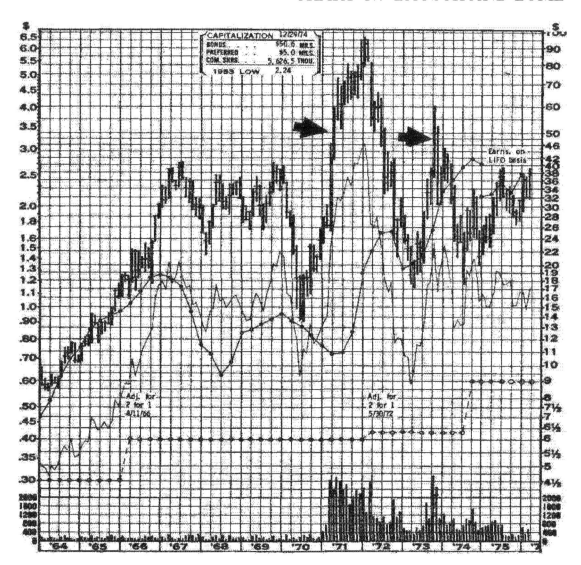

The announcement in 1971 that this manufacturer of optical products would produce a new soft contact lens resulted in a superperformance move in the stock's price and a big volume of trading, as shown at the bottom of the chart.

Chart by Securities Research Company

become vigorous and strong. Some companies have reached maturity; their growth is slow or has stopped. A few are declining in their old age; and a few railroads that were born in the mid-1800s are now dying.

Any investor looking for large capital gains in the stock market should look for companies that are in the growth stage of the life cycle. These are usually companies that have been established for a few years; they have been in existence long enough so that their chances of survival are pretty good. But they are usually fairly small companies, with comparatively few shares of common stock issued, usually under ten million.

The percentage growth of sales and earnings, and also the stock's price, can usually be much more rapid for a five-million-share company than for a hundred-and-fifty-million-share company, particularly if an appealing new product is being manufactured and large companies do not have the advantage of patents and established distribution channels for that particular product.

An expression of the rapid growth potential of small companies as compared with large ones is found in the exponential curve or S-Curve. The growth curve, shown in Chart 18, moves from the horizontal, swings upward in fast growth, then levels off in maturity. Most large companies are now in the slow-growth mature stage. Many smaller, young companies are in the dynamic rapid-growth stage.

Mature Companies

There has been a considerable amount of investment advice over the years that has advocated buying quality. "Stick to the blue chips," it said, "and you won't be hurt." But the record reveals that an investor can be hurt severely if he buys a blue chip at the wrong time. And even if he does not lose financially, he usually has gained very little, particularly considering the risks he has taken. The Dow Jones industrial average consists of

CHART 18. THE S-CURVE IN THE DOW JONES INDUSTRIAL AVERAGE

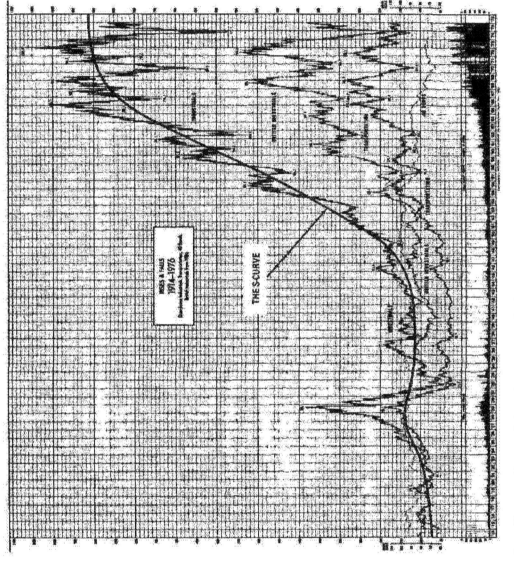

The S-Curve, or exponential curve of growth, is a curve that grows by a multiplying figure, or exponent. The S-Curve gradually rises from the horizontal, then swings rapidly upward during a period of fast growth. The curve levels off again during maturity.

This chart of the Dow Jones industrial average, which is comprised of thirty large, mature corporations, shows the exponential curve gradually rising from the horizontal in the 1940s and early 1950s. Since 1965 the Dow Jones industrial average has leveled off, indicating a period of maturity.

Chart by Securities Research Company

113

some of the biggest, strongest corporations in the country; included are companies like AT&T, duPont, General Electric, General Motors, Goodyear, U. S. Steel. Most are considered blue chip investments. Yet the stock prices of most of these companies reached their peaks years ago.

For perspective, let's look back at some stocks available to the investor in 1952. There was General Motors with 87,000,000 shares, General Electric with 28,800,000. Today General Motors has 285,500,000 shares outstanding, U. S. Steel has 54,000,000, and General Electric has. 90,700,000.

But there were also some much smaller companies available in 1952. There was Avon Products with only 596,000 shares; today Avon Products has 57,800,000 shares. Polaroid was also available in 1952 with 404,000 shares. There was also a small company named Haloid that made photographic papers. It had 189,000 shares of stock. The capitalization of the company, now called Xerox, has now grown to 78,900,000 shares. IBM's capitalization has grown from 3,000,000 shares in 1952 to about 145,000,000 in 1974. So, although the companies that were large in 1952 continued to grow, their growth was exceeded many times over by much smaller companies which were little known at that time.

Use Caution When Selecting Growth Stocks

In choosing growth-stage companies, it is necessary to be very selective. Stock prices can be pushed up quickly because of a good promotion or story that usually describes impressive plans for future development. But in the long run stock prices are based on earning power. So the story has to begin to come true or else disillusioned investors will begin to sell their stock and drive down the price. As long as the story is coming true through satisfactorily increasing earnings, most investors will continue to hold their stock. Separating fact from fancy is the big job of investors who are searching for growth, and for superperformance price action based on growth.

Good Management Is Vital

Avoid new stock issues. This is one of the surest ways to lose your money. The story might sound terrific, but it takes more than a story to build a successful business. It takes highly capable management and a lot of money to carry the company through its development stages.

Companies that are in the growth stage of the life cycle often have more momentum than large, mature, established companies. A few years ago the president of Xerox, Joe Wilson, stated that it was very important for his company to maintain its momentum. The image presented by a company is as important as that presented by an individual. Momentum in a company indicates that it is on the move, progressing, with steadily increasing sales and earnings. Momentum indicates an alert, aggressive management willing to listen to new ideas and to try out new methods. Momentum implies that a company spends money on research and introduces new products resulting from that research. A company with momentum is rewarded for its good performance by investors, who often are willing to pay a premium price for the stock of a company in motion.

Turnaround Situations

Sometimes companies are reinvigorated, often because a new management team has taken over. When this occurs, the result is a turnaround: A company that has been sliding downhill begins again on a new, upward growth cycle.

In the late 1950s and early 1960s Chrysler Corporation had the image of a company about to go out of business. Year after year the company's share of the automobile market declined. Dealerships were being closed. Chrysler's share of the market continued in a decline. A large part of the problem appeared to be the unattractive styling of some car models, with a resulting decline in popularity and sales. Eventually, a dynamic new management team was brought in to rescue the company. They began to improve the situation almost immediately. Chrysler was a typical turnaround situation in early 1963 when I purchased the stock. The price had already started to rise rapidly in typical superperformance action. By the end of 1963 it had quadrupled; the climb continued through 1964, finally terminating near the end of the year. Chart 19, a twelve-year chart of Chrysler, shows the strong price superperformance phase that occurred from the 1962 bear market bottom until late 1964.

The superperformance phase included two 2 for 1 stock splits. The rise was propelled by increases in earnings. Per share earnings were $5.46 in 1964 and $4.19 in 1963, compared with $1.74 in 1962, $.30 in 1961, $.87 in 1960, and deficits in 1959 and 1958. The turnaround was brought about by the new management's cost-cutting measures and increased sales.

Management changes are frequently the forerunner of turnarounds. One approach to successful speculation is to keep close watch on companies undergoing this type of change.

A Comparison of Two Growth Stocks

Some investors buy stocks while others sell because they anticipate the future in different ways. Some sell because when they look a few months ahead they see a possible recession coming. Others, looking farther ahead, buy because they believe that the price of the stock already discounts a possible recession. They are anticipating the business recovery, and the vast growth of revenues and earning power that they see in some companies.

CHART 19. CHRYSLER

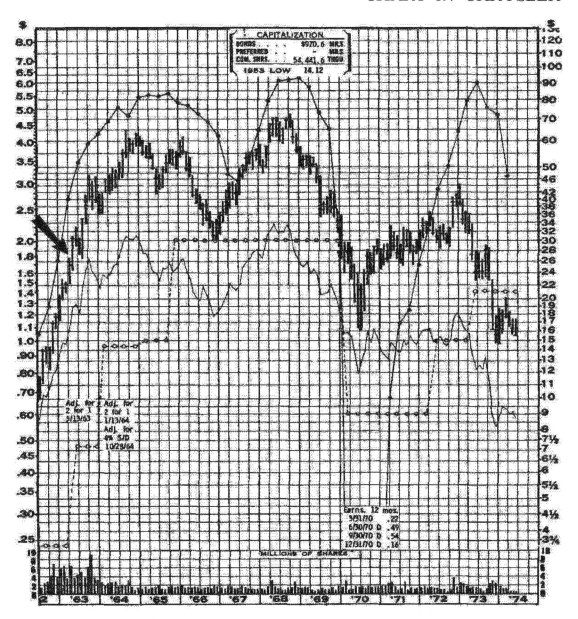

The chart illustrates the turnaround that began in 1962 when
new management assumed control of the company. The arrow
points to the superperformance price phase. The earnings of
the company have been sensitive to business cycles, resulting in
volatile stock-price performance.

Chart by Securities Research Company

I recall knowing of some specific companies with such obvious growth potential that at the time I wondered why other investors did not seem to view the stock with the same enthusiasm that I did. In 1953 I purchased the stock of an unlisted company that had a rapidly expanding chain of popular restaurants. It was a capably managed company and appeared to have vast potential for growth. Yet for a long time the stock remained relatively quiet. It appeared to me that hardly anyone else was interested in the company, or had even heard of it. That company was Hot Shoppes, Inc., now known as Marriott Corporation. Today it has a chain of hotels and owns about five hundred restaurants. Sometimes an investor just has to wait and wait for other investors to become aware of a good opportunity. It is a matter of being too far ahead of the crowd. There are times when an abundance of patience is required.

Growth potential can sometimes be a very elusive quality. Many companies that have been referred to in the financial press year after year as glamour stocks do not appear to have nearly as much growth as numerous unpublicized companies. Compare the performance of Polaroid in Chart 20 with that of Kresge (S.S.) in Chart 21. Polaroid has been the publicized company, the glamour stock. Polaroid Corporation's stock for many years was given a very high price/earnings multiple by investors. For at least a decade the stock had a P/E consistently over 30, frequently over 50, and sometimes as high as 90. Yet Polaroid's earnings trend has often been erratic, as is shown by the chart. From 1967 to 1975 there was virtually no increase in earnings. Polaroid holds hundreds of patents in the field of instant, one-step photography. In Polaroid's process, the materials required for developing and printing are part of the film. This permits the person taking photographs to obtain a completed print from the camera within seconds. It is this potential that has appealed to investors. Moreover, the company has continued growing even though net income has remained quite static. Revenues have increased consistently. It has been research and the cost of developing new photographic systems that have depressed earnings. At some point in the future the stock's growth potential is likely to be seen again, as it was between 1964 and 1968 when the price of the stock rose more than 600 percent in a strong superperformance phase.

Kresge, on the other hand, has not been as highly publicized and has less frequently been referred to as a glamour stock. All it has done is to grow steadily year after year in the relatively unglamourous and highly competitive field of variety store merchandising. Kresge's net income has increased each year since 1962; gross revenues have increased steadily for an even longer period. The company's K-Mart chain has become the largest discount chain in the country.

In 1963, when Kresge stock began its first superperformance price phase, the company had only 5,518,000 shares of stock. The P/E ratio was about 14. So an ideal combination was present; a reasonably priced stock in a small company that had *vast growth potential* and increasing *earning power*.

Anticipate Growth

With some companies it is possible to anticipate strong growth in revenues and earnings for many years in the future. The gross revenues of IBM, for example, were $410,000,000 in 1953, $2,863,000,000 in 1963, and $12,675,000,000 in 1974. Xerox had gross revenues of $268,000,000 in 1964 and $3,576,400,000 in 1974. In the early 1950s it was therefore possible to see that vast growth ahead for IBM, just as it was possible to see the growth potential of Xerox in the early 1960s. Many investors did see the vast potential of these companies and acted. Vast growth potential is one of the reasons these companies have been popular, which has resulted in their having high P/E ratios.

CHART 20. POLAROID

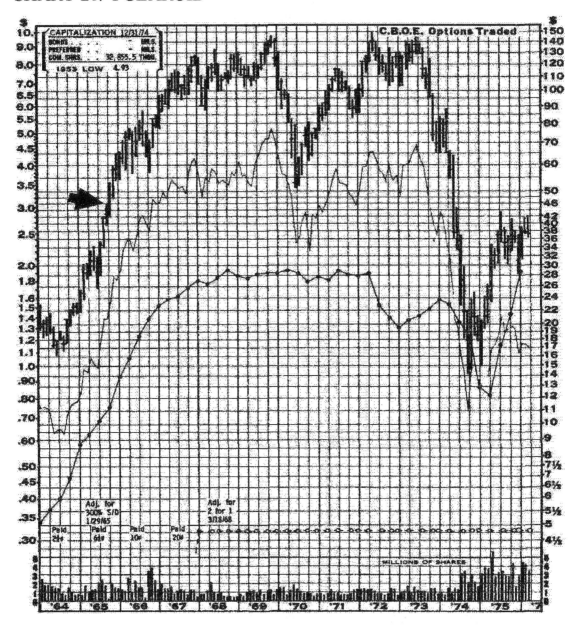

For many years investors have seen vast growth potential in Polaroid's new photographic processes, and the stock has had a high P/E ratio. However, since 1968 the earnings trend has been generally flat. A superperformance phase began in 1964.

Chart by Securities Research Company

120

CHART 21. KRESGE(S.S.)

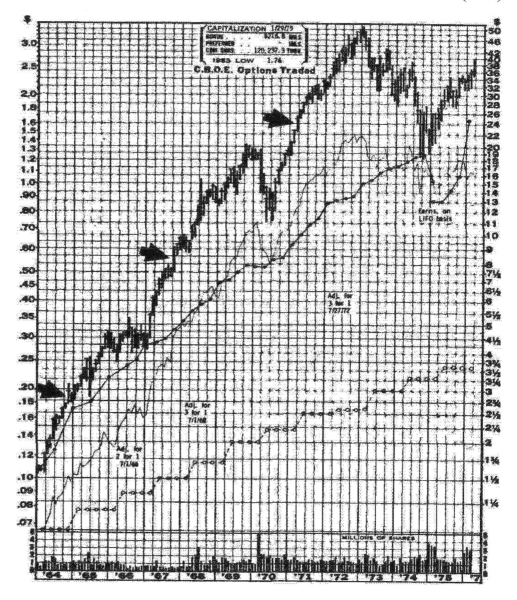

This stock of the leading discount retailer has experienced
three superperformance price phases. The first phase began
in 1963 and lasted until 1966; the stock approximately quadrupled in price. The second phase began in early 1967 and ended
in late 1969; the price again quadrupled. The third phase, during
which the price quadrupled again, began near the 1970 bear
market bottom and lasted until January 1973. Except for one
quarter in 1969 ;the earnings have consistently increased from
quarter to quarter. The stock's price has increased even faster
than earnings, and there has been a large expansion in the P/E
ratio, as can be seen on the chart by the increasing separation
of the vertical price range bars from the earnings lines.
Chart by Securities Research Company

Even if it is necessary to wait a number of years for a stock to be recognized, eventually such patience can prove to be very rewarding. Your only real alternative is to find another stock that will have superperformance price action sooner.

Earnings Explosions

Earnings explosions are often of great significance because they call attention to newly developed earning power. Recently I ran across a small clipping I had torn from a local newspaper in the summer of 1963. The clipping reads: "Xerox Corporation in 6 months ended June 30 earned $10,327,031 or $2.66 a share vs. $5,658,165 or $1.74 in 1962 period." That is an example of an earnings explosion: a large sudden increase in the profitability of a company.

The earnings explosion occurred just after Xerox introduced its new copiers, and the earnings increase was directly traceable to revenues from the new copiers.

At about the same time in 1963 I purchased another stock that was beginning to look very interesting, Syntex Corporation, shown in Chart 22. Earlier in the year Syntex had sold at under $12 a share. By January 1964 it had reached as high as $190 per share before heavy institutional selling caused a reaction. One of the strongest forces propelling the price increase was the rumor, later confirmed, of a large increase in earnings. In this case the earnings for the 1963 fiscal year were more than quadruple the earnings for fiscal 1962. Of even greater importance than reported earnings, however, was the expectation in the minds of speculators that future earnings would be even larger. Syntex at that time was one of two companies pioneering the development of birth control pills. Investors could anticipate a very large market and increased earnings for the future. Thus, the expectation of large future earnings caused a buyers' stampede for the stock.

CHART 22 SYNTEX

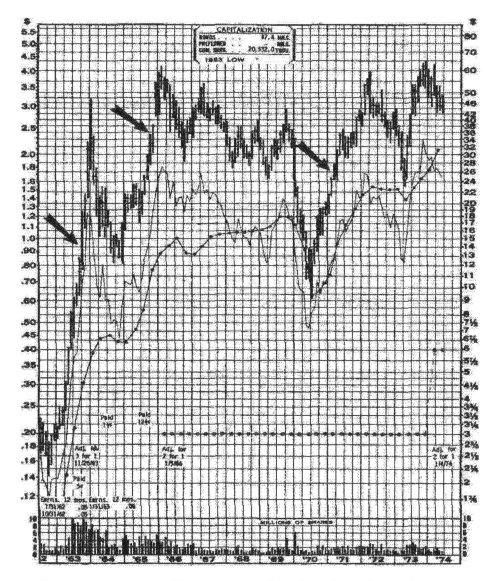

Syntex was a small company that developed a unique new patent-protected product, birth control pills, which had vast growth potential. In 1963 the company had a big increase in earnings and also received extensive publicity. The stock has had strong sponsorship and institutional interest. The arrows indicate superperformance phases.

Chart by Securities Research Company

123

Be Skeptical of Reported Earnings

Many investors act on the basis of reported earnings, even when the earnings might exist only in the imagination of some creative accountant, or be of a merely temporary nature. Many of these investment errors are caused by the fact that companies report their quarterly earnings to the financial press, where the information is printed and widely distributed. But the quarterly figures are unaudited. Moreover, no details are given that might help investors to evaluate the figures and determine whether a reported earnings increase indicates a new trend or merely a temporary situation.

During the 1970 recession, when stock prices were severely depressed, another action occurred. Corporate treasurers suddenly became ultraconservative, writing down inventories, buildings, research projects, and future costs by setting up reserves. That approach lowered 1970 earnings, but every dollar charged off against 1970 added that much to future profits. Corporate officers have justified such an action by stating that it helps shareholders. When write-offs are concentrated in a single year it assists the stock in rebounding the next year. These accounting practices probably reinforce the cyclical action of the earnings of many companies and the price action of the stock. Some earnings increases are cyclical in nature and might not indicate newly developed earning power.

Reported Earnings Depend on Accounting Procedures

If an investor is interested in particular groups, such as oil or steel companies, he should keep in mind that all companies do not necessarily report their earnings in the same manner. They might use different accounting procedures, which of course makes it very difficult to compare stocks. Among oil companies, for instance, some defer the cost of drilling expenses over the expected life of the properties, while others do not. In the case of large oil companies, millions of dollars are involved. It points up the fact that reported profits and earnings should often be regarded with skepticism.

The important question for the investor to keep in mind is: "Are the earnings going to continue to increase in the future?" The best clues are likely to be found in the nature of the business, the plans of management, and the trends in the volume of sales and revenues. The quality of earnings increases, in other words, must be evaluated.

Higher Earnings Are Usually Anticipated

But how about earnings that are uncomplicated by manipulation, that are higher simply because the company had a much more profitable year? Let's suppose the earnings are reported and they have doubled. The stock should go up in price, right? No, not necessarily. Not if a dozen mutual fund managers had expected earnings to triple, not merely double. They would be disappointed and might decide to sell. Other investors who had predicted the earnings increase might decide to sell on the news. Reports of large increases in earnings have their biggest impact when they come as a *surprise.* When that happens, almost everyone has an opportunity to participate in the resulting rise. Being able to interpret the effect that an earnings report will have on the market is very important. And even more significant is the light it might cast on the company's prospects for continued future profits. Earning power, real and potential, is the most important feature to look for.

Earning Trends Affect Superperformance Price Action

My review of the long-term charts of 1,018 stocks revealed that increased earnings trends often are important influences in superperformance stock-price moves. Approximately 38 percent of the stock-price moves coincided with or briefly followed large increases in the reported quarterly earnings. An additional 28 percent of the moves appeared to be associated with relatively moderate earnings increases, but in about 34 percent of the price moves no correlation could be made. There were many cases of declining prices during periods of rising earnings, particularly when bear market conditions prevailed. The long-term chart histories of prices and earnings indicate that investors overreact to reported or expected earnings increases.

The Role Future Earnings Play in Stock Prices

The movement of individual stock prices, then, is related in the long run to the earnings anticipated in the future. When certain influences are present, such as important news developments or changes in national monetary policies, virtually the entire stock market moves in unison in a bullish or bearish direction because investors anticipate the influence that the new development will have on future earnings.

But future earnings have not always been so important in determining the value of a stock. Benjamin Graham and David L. Dodd in their book *Security Analysis,* first published in 1934, pointed out that the trend of earnings concept for valuation developed during the latter stages of the bull market culminating in 1929. Formerly, investment in common stocks was based on three elements: a suitable and established dividend return, a stable and adequate earnings record, and asset values. This approach to common-stock investment was considered inadequate because past earnings and dividends could no longer be considered an index of future earnings and dividends. During the 1920s change in the fortunes of companies was rapid, as it is today. As a result, the idea became dominant that the value of

126

common stock depended on what it would earn in the future, and a good stock would show a rising trend of earnings. This change in the method of evaluating common stocks resulted in a blurring of the distinctions between investment and speculation, since emphasis was placed on the enhancement of principal instead of on the dividend received from the investment.

Evaluate Reported Earnings

The investor must base his decision to invest or not to invest on much more information than merely reported earnings. He must find out what caused the increase in reported earnings and he must determine whether or not the increase can be expected to continue. A large increase in reported earnings can be a one-time thing. It might result from tax credits or the sale of property or other assets. Recently one of the nation's largest steel corporations reported a large increase in earnings, but this was principally caused by a change in accounting methods. In another example, in early 1974 the Securities and Exchange Commission charged Avis, Inc., with mailing shareholders a false and misleading report for 1973's first quarter; Avis had failed to disclose that about 70 percent of its earnings had come from vehicle sales.

Since the trend of earnings is followed closely by the majority of investors, most managements report earnings quarterly and the information is dutifully reported in the financial press. The price of the company's stock usually reacts quickly to quarterly earnings reports if the announced figures are different from those that had been anticipated. But the details on which the quarterly results are based might not be available for study until many, many months later. Thus, investors can be and frequently are misled by the quarterly earnings reported by company managements.

The most creative accountants have mastered the

technique of showing minimal earnings to the Internal Revenue people and exploding earnings to the investing public. This sleight-of-hand approach calls for bullish publicity for potential stock purchasers but a large dose of reality later, when income taxes have to be reported. There have been too many people, both in corporate management and on Wall Street, who have regarded the investor as a sucker to be taken. They stopped selling the Brooklyn Bridge to visitors many years ago. The obvious reason is that the quick-buck artists discovered a more sophisticated and a much more lucrative place: Wall Street.

So try to anticipate earnings for specific companies and for the general market. Try to determine the trend and the extent of the increase or decrease in earnings. But remain skeptical and investigate reported figures. Select stocks that seem to be undervalued in relation to prospects for growth.

Chapter 10
Look for Expandable Price/Earnings Ratios

Most superperformance price moves are caused not by developments such as increased earnings, but rather by overreaction of investors to those developments. The overreaction can be measured quite accurately by comparing the increase in the price to the increase in earnings—that is, by the expansion in the P/E ratio. Some of the biggest stock market profits are made by going along with the crowd while it pushes the price of a stock higher and higher in nonstop optimism. Superperformance price moves occur in a stock when large numbers of investors all think alike and cause a buying stampede. Stock prices rise rapidly and everyone is bullish, expecting even higher prices. Supply and demand forces operate. Many people want to buy and few want to sell, so the bidding escalates rapidly.

Sometimes the quickest profits are obtained during these periods of optimism in very active stocks that everyone seems to be aware of and many people are trading. But with this type of stock it is important to be in the action early. Cautious investors often delay their purchase until they are absolutely certain that they are right in buying a stock. It is often at this point that the stock, which has been going up in price for some time, is due for a reaction. Do not be too late in joining the action; it is also important not to overstay a position that has turned stale or has started to decline. Be alert for turns or changes in investor psychology. For your own protection it is discreet to use stop-loss orders if the price of a stock has risen rapidly.

A stop-loss order is an instruction to a stockbroker to sell a specific number of shares of stock if the price declines to a designated level. The broker will try to sell the stock at the designated price. Stop-loss orders are intended to minimize losses. This step is particularly recommended if you are not able to follow the market closely.

Just as there are times to go along with the bullish enthusiasm of the crowd, there are also times to leave, to stand aside. The time to sell is when the bullish drive is beginning to lose its momentum, to turn stale.

Price superperformance phases do not last indefinitely. Most of them last only a couple of years, then the stock reacts into a downtrend or sideways price action. The prevailing mood of investors changes, often slowly, from bullish optimism, to doubt and apprehension, to bearish pessimism, and finally to panic as the decline accelerates. As with unbounded optimism, never underestimate the power of negative thinking. Fear and pessimism become so overwhelming at times that even the strongest, most bullish-looking stocks are caught up in the selling deluge. The speculative mood of investors appears to move in waves of pessimism and optimism that are based on actual economic or political conditions but which greatly amplify those conditions. When the national economy becomes strong, the stock market often becomes even more bullish than is justified by the facts. When the economy turns down and forecasters begin warning of a possible recession, the investors become even more pessimistic than is justified and they sell stocks down to bargain-price levels. Investment psychology often loses its logic and becomes emotional. The news media play a particularly important role in developing moods of mass optimism or pessimism.

The P/E ratio reflects the enthusiastic optimism or gloomy pessimism of investors. At one period in 1961 the P/E ratio of the Dow Jones industrials hit 24; at the end of 1973 the ratio was 10; and in late 1974 it was as low as 6. The change in the ratio for many individual stocks was much greater. In early January 1973, the Dow Jones industrial average reached a bull market peak of 1,067. At that time the P/E ratios of some stocks reached very high multiples, but by 1974 the P/E ratios of the same stocks had contracted to lower multiples. This contraction in the P/E ratio occurred while earnings were rising. But the psychological setting had changed, for 1973 was the year of Watergate and the energy crisis, and 1974 brought fear of an approaching recession. So the real change occurred in the psychology of investors, from a mood of confidence and optimism to one of doubt and pessimism. The P/E ratio reflects that change in attitude.

Psychology and Stock Prices

Of all the forces that influence stock prices, mass fear and mass greed can often be the most dominant. Strong psychological forces can move prices in individual stocks, and the stock market as a whole, faster and faster upward and downward than is justified by the news that usually gives the impetus to the move. By causing price moves to go to high and low extremes, psychological forces create excellent selling and buying opportunities for alert investors.

It is unrealistic always to be optimistic or always to be pessimistic. There is a time for optimism and there is a time for pessimism. More important than your mood is your sensitivity to whether the crowd is optimistic or pessimistic. The rewards are few if you are optimistic while the crowd is selling in waves of pessimism. The crowd may be wrong, but you cannot fight the crowd by yourself. If you try to buck the stampede, you will be trampled. If you buy a stock too early during a period of highly emotional selling, you will soon discover that you have a loss, and perhaps a large one. The time to be contrary, to sell or to pick up bargains, is after an emotional binge of mass optimism or pessimism has lost momentum and a reversal is imminent. Soon others will realize that the future is not as bleak or as rosy as it had appeared. News developments, particularly the way they are reported in the media, frequently are the biggest influence in creating the dominant mood. To a considerable degree prices are made by emotions and by the shifting attitudes of large numbers of investors.

Emotions also play a very significant role in selecting a stock for purchase. The image of a company is projected in its type of business and in its name. If we name a company Planetary Explorations Unlimited, for example, to start in the business of exploring the universe, it will create a different impression in the mind of a prospective investor than, say, a company named Consolidated Concrete.

Establishing Stock Values

In the late 1940s, when I was a graduate student taking business courses at Columbia University, I recall that one professor, lecturing on the determination of values, explained that a piece of property is worth as much as someone is willing to pay you for it. So it is with common stock. Find stocks for which you think someone will be willing to pay you a higher price at some time in the future. This approach is applicable to any type of investment—in a diamond, a painting, a bushel of corn or wheat, a house, a piece of land, or a share of common stock. The market price of the item reflects the psychological factors—the extremes of optimism and pessimism—that can cause the value of an item to vary widely, sometimes in just a few hours or days. When the market value of an item is plummeting, it reveals that the fear many people have of lower values for their property is stronger than their hopes for higher prices.

There are several methods for establishing the theoretical value of a stock as compared with its selling price in the market. One is the company's book value, which is determined by adding up the company's assets, subtracting the liabilities, and dividing by the number of common shares outstanding. The large discrepancy that exists between marketplace value and asset value is clearly pointed up by the closed-end investment companies that have been priced for years at substantial discounts from their net asset value. During bear markets the discount expands; in bull markets it contracts.

In the early years of this century assets were usually given greater weight than they are now and investors traditionally bought stocks for their dividends. Today a company's earning power, particularly its future earning power, is the most important consideration.

Another approach to establishing value is to compare the dividends available from income-paying stocks with the yield available from bonds and other types of investments. Until 1958 bond yields were considerably lower than the dividends being paid by the companies comprising the Dow Jones industrials. During the years prior to 1956 the average yield of forty bonds fluctuated between 3 and 4 percent. But, beginning in 1956, bond yields began to climb irregularly, rising to above 10 percent in 1974. Dividends paid by the stocks were above 6.5 percent during most of 1951. Stock yields declined steadily after 1951. In 1958 the yields from bonds became higher than from stocks, and bond yields have been higher ever since, by a wide margin. The erosion in the value of the dollar through inflation has been responsibile for the large increase in bond yields. In more recent years inflation has been the major cause for the steady price decline of income-type stocks, such as the utilities and large, mature companies that are not growing rapidly but are also not increasing their dividends sufficiently to justify their purchase as income-type investments.

Other methods of establishing the value of stocks have been developed, including one which assumes that the value of a security is equal to the present worth of all future payments. Another method attempts to estimate future earnings and dividends for a specific period of time, such as ten years. The investor must believe that a fair rate of return, called the discount rate, is a certain percentage, say 9 percent. Thus, if a stock declined in price to yield 9 percent, it would be priced to yield what that investor considers to be a fair rate of return. Sometimes the expected dividend rate is combined with an estimated rate of price appreciation to establish a value for the stock. "Total return" is the term used for what your investment earns annually on a combined yield and price-change basis.

Problems in Establishing Values

The problem with attempting to establish a stock's value using these methods is that certain assumptions about the future are made. It is assumed, for instance, that earnings will continue to grow at a predicted rate, that dividends will continue and will be increased at a certain rate over a specified period of time, or that the stock's price will appreciate at a certain rate. But there are comparatively few stocks that are really suitable for these methods of establishing value. For most companies it is very difficult to establish a rate at which earnings will grow, and even more difficult to predict a rate of price appreciation. The desire to establish value in this manner has caused many companies to manipulate or "manage" their earnings so that they show a steady rate of earnings increase. The managed earnings might or might not reflect reality. So one problem with placing a theoretical worth on stock based on its intrinsic value is that the intrinsic value for most stocks cannot be precisely determined. How can anyone determine with precision the future competition that a product will encounter? Distant future earnings and company developments cannot be accurately forecast.

Market Price vs. Inherent Value

There often appears to be little relationship between the price of a stock and its inherent value. Stocks that are overpriced relative to their inherent value often have severe price declines sooner or later, but many of them remain in an overpriced state for years before the price reaction occurs. In a similar way, some stocks of companies in unglamourous industries are frequently depressed in price, as compared with stocks in general. Throughout the late 1960s and early 1970s when most stock prices and the market averages were soaring, the steel industry stocks remained depressed. The mere fact that a stock is depressed in price relative to its inherent value does not necessarily mean that an adjustment will be made and that the stock's price will rise. The stock can remain depressed for many, many years. Finding "value" is not enough, by itself, to assure that a specific investment is good. The book values of stocks are relatively stable in comparison with their large fluctuations in market price.

The large disparity between the book value per share of a stock and its market value is illustrated by the following table.

Table 3

	1971		1974	
	book value	market value	book value	market value
Polaroid	17	$117^1/s$-76	19	$88^1/i$>-$14V_8$
U. S. Steel	67	$35^1/_8$-25	72	$48^1/_2$-$35^3/8$
IBM	57	$365^3/4$-$283V_4$	60	254-150^1£
Xerox	13	$126^3/4$-$84^3/4$	18	$127^1/s$-49
Lehigh Portland Cement	25	17-$12^5/s$	31	21 V_8-8
Natomas	31	$101^3/8$-$43^3/4$	34	73 V_8-$34^5/s$

In the examples of U.S. Steel and Lehigh Portland Cement the book value per share of the stock has remained consistently above the market price of the stock. In the other examples shown in the table the market price has stayed consistently much higher than the book value per share, with the exception of Polaroid in 1974. Not only is there little or no relationship between the book value per share of the stock and its market value, but the market value itself has fluctuated widely, in response to levels of company earnings, but more so in response to investor optimism or pessimism. The latter is effectively measured by the P/E ratio.

A tabulation in Standard & Poor's June 1975 *Stock Guide* of the 292 largest companies based on their 1974 net income showed that 120 of the companies had a higher book value than market value, while 127 companies had higher market value than book value.

Examples of companies that had much higher market prices than book values included:

Table 4

International Business Machines:			book value 32% of market price		
Eastman Kodak	it	ii	20%"	ii	tt
Xerox	ft	ii	29%"	it	ft
Dow Chemical	it	ii	23%"	it	it
Minnesota Mining &Mfg.	it	It	22%"	ft	it
Procter & Gamble	ii	it	24%"	tt	it
Weyerhauser	ii	it	28%"	ft	it
American Home Products	it	it	10%"	tt	ft
Coca-Cola	ii	it	18%"	tt	ti
Johnson & Johnson	ii	it	18%"	tt	tt
Lilly (Eli) & Co.	it	ii	15%"	ft	it
Schlumberger	it	it	14%"	tt	it

Company						
Halliburton	book value	25%	of market price			
Burroughs	"	"	28%	"	"	"
Schering-Plough	"	"	15%	"	"	"
Bristol Myers	"	"	24%	"	"	"
Avon Products	"	"	17%	"	"	"
Kresge (S.S.)	"	"	29%	"	"	"
McDonald's	"	"	14%	"	"	"

Examples of companies that had much higher book values than market prices included:

Table 5

Company						
Consolidated Edison:	book value	293%	of market price			
Signal Cos.	"	"	234%	"	"	"
Republic Steel	"	"	260%	"	"	"
Lykes Youngstown	"	"	327%	"	"	"
Santa Fe Industries	"	"	232%	"	"	"
Southern Pacific	"	"	336%	"	"	"
Anaconda Co.	"	"	361%	"	"	"
Seaboard Coast Line	"	"	314%	"	"	"
General Tire & Rubber	"	"	209%	"	"	"
Wheeling Pittsburgh	"	"	357%	"	"	"
Woolworth (F. W.)	"	"	202%	"	"	"
Consumers Power	"	"	244%	"	"	"
1C Industries	"	"	389%	"	"	"

A review of the long-term charts of the stocks on Tables 4 and 5 revealed that the stocks on the first table—the stocks that have a much higher market price per share than book value—are also stocks that have had consistently rising earnings and a price history that generally followed the upward earnings trend. They were also stocks that were heavily favored by institutional investors. They have had high price/earnings ratios as well as high price/assets ratios.

The stocks on the second table—the stocks with high book values per share relative to their market price per share—are stocks that have had erratic earnings and price records. They have not been favorites of institutional investors.

It is apparent, by comparing these two stock groups, that stock selections have been made based on good earnings trends. Large assets have been less important in determining purchases. Will the investment selection pattern change? In the future will investors, particularly the institutional investors now dominating common stock investment, buy stocks on the basis of book value instead of earnings? Probably not. Stock selections will probably continue to be based primarily on the outlook for the earnings of individual companies.

Market Price vs. Dividends

A review of the long-term charts, which show the level of dividend payments as well as earnings and price histories, also revealed little relationship between the dividend level and the stock's price. In numerous instances stocks have had declining price trends while their dividends were being increased. There are very few cases in which a dividend increase appears to have caused a price increase. The lack of relationship between price and dividend payout can be observed on two earlier charts—Dow Jones Utility Average, Chart 7, and American Telephone and Telegraph, Chart 8—and on International Business Machines, Chart 25, which appears toward the end of this chapter.

The investment manager of a large university endowment reported that during 1974's severe bear market eighteen of the twenty-eight stocks in the university's portfolio increased their dividends. But the portfolio decreased 40.5 percent in value during the year. The investment manager stated that the university had erred in maintaining a fully invested position, but acknowledged the lack of timing ability.

Estimating Price/Earnings Ratios

After you have estimated the earnings to be expected by a company, it is necessary to estimate a P/E ratio for the stock. How many times its earnings do you expect the stock might sell for? If you estimate that a company will have earnings of five dollars a share and that it could conservatively have a P/E ratio of 10, then the stock should be expected to sell for fifty dollars at some time in future months. If the current price of the stock is only seventeen dollars, then the stock might be considered a good buy if the primary trend of the market is upward and is expected to continue climbing.

In my review of the long-term charts I discovered that there were a few stocks whose earnings were increasing at a faster rate than their price. They were the exceptions. In 464 of the 589 superperformance moves the P/E ratio at the end of the move was higher than at the beginning.

P/E ratios expand to higher multiples when the future looks very good; they contract to lower multiples when the future looks bleak or uncertain. P/E's are sensitive measurements of mass psychology. The evidence indicates, therefore, that investor psychology is just the opposite of what it should be for successful investment, since P/E ratios have been high at the end of superperformance moves. But it is after a stock price has moved upward for two or three years that caution and a low P/E ratio are called for, since it is at this time that a price reaction is most likely to occur. And even the very best stocks have price reactions.

My study of the long-term charts also indicated that most superperformance price moves begin when P/E ratios are at a relatively low level, or in stocks that have relatively low P/E's. Only about 10 percent of the moves began in stocks that had P/E ratios above 20. It is very difficult for a high P/E ratio, such as 45, to double to 90. But it is relatively easy for a stock with a P/E ratio of 10 to double to 20 or even to triple to 30. Stocks with high P/E ratios are more dependent on increased earnings to bring about higher prices, rather than expanding P/E multiples.

P/E ratios reflect the popularity of a stock. If the future earnings of a company look good, the P/E ratio is likely to be high, perhaps 20 or 30. If the future of the company appears to be fabulous and investors are highly optimistic, the ratio might be 50 or 60. But if there are indications of future problems, perhaps portending an earnings decline, the P/E ratio might decline to 10 or less.

So when the earnings of a company are predicted to double, do not expect the price to double. If the P/E of the company is exceptionally low at the time the estimate is made, the result might be that the price will more than double. If a share of stock is selling for five dollars and earnings were one dollar a share, its P/E is 5. If earnings are expected to be two dollars, the optimism generated by this news is likely to cause the P/E to expand, perhaps to 10 or 20 or even higher if the rate of earnings increase is expected to continue. Thus a stock earning two dollars a share might be expected to sell for twenty dollars with a P/E of 10, or forty dollars if the P/E expands to 20.

However, take a theoretical example of a stock earning a dollar a share that is expected to double earnings to two dollars a share. The stock, however, has been selling for eighty dollars, with a P/E of 80. It is therefore unrealistic to expect the stock to more than double in price. The increased earnings are already discounted in the high price of the stock.

In market sell-offs, lower earnings are usually less responsible for lower stock prices than are psychological influences resulting in lower P/E ratios. Thus, a company might have earnings of $8 a share. With its stock selling for $160, the P/E ratio is 20. But let's assume that the national economy has entered a recession and that the company's anticipated earnings for next year are expected to decline to $4 a share. If the price of the stock declines at the same ratio as the earnings, it might decline to 80, retaining the P/E ratio of 20. But because of the effect of mass pessimism among stockholders, the P/E ratio might contract to 15 or less. The result might be a stock price of $60 or lower.

The P/E ratio can also be expressed as an earnings yield. For example, if a stock earned five dollars during the past year and the stock's price is one hundred dollars, the P/E ratio is 20; the earnings yield is 5 percent. If the stock's price is fifty dollars, the P/E ratio is 10 and the earnings yield is 10 percent.

McDonald's shown on Chart 23, and International Flavors and Fragrances, on Chart 24, are good illustrations of companies that have had expanding P/E multiples. McDonald's P/E ratio expanded from 11 in 1966 to 90 in 1972. International Flavors and Fragrances also revealed its steadily increasing popularity by having an expanding P/E ratio.

The Influence of Price/Earnings Ratios

A sizable psychological impact may have occurred in 1972 when the financial pages of newspapers began printing the P/E ratios of stocks. Until then this information was not readily available, and it is unlikely that many individual investors consistently went to the trouble of computing the ratios. Of greater significance, perhaps, is the ability to see at a glance how the P/E ratios of various stocks compare. One effect of having the P/E ratios seen daily by millions of investors is that

CHART 23. McDONALD'S

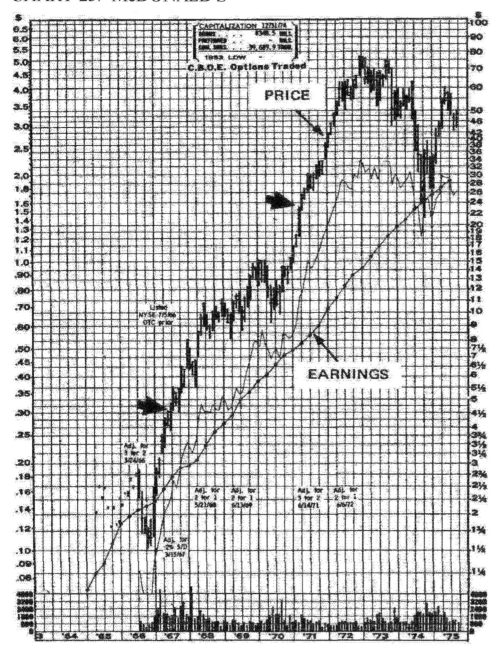

The chart of this nationwide restaurant chain shows a P/E
ratio that has expanded, or increased to high multiples. When
the Price Range bars and Earnings line coincide, the price is at
fifteen times earnings. When the price is above the Earnings
line, the ratio of price to earnings is greater than fifteen times
earnings; when below, it is less. In 1972 the P/E ratio of
McDonald's increased to as high as 90. The arrows point to
superperformance.

Chart by Securities Research Company

CHART 24. INTERNATIONAL FLAVORS AND FRAGRANCES

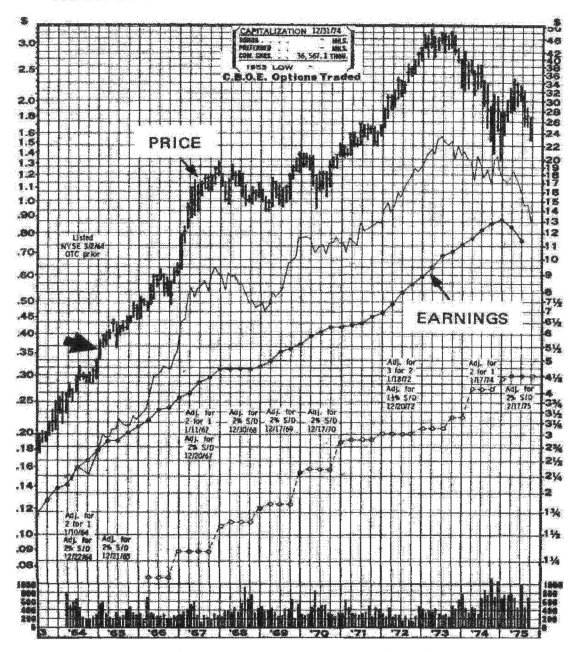

The increase in the P/E ratio of this stock is shown by the widening gap between the Price Bars and the Earnings line. The P/E expanded from 25 at the end of 1963 to 75 at the end of 1972. In late 1973 the stock's price began to decline long before the downturn in earnings that occurred at the end of 1974. IFF's customers are the cosmetics, detergent, and beverage industries.

Chart by Securities Research Company

143

they are likely to be more cautious about purchasing a stock with a high P/E ratio when they see hundreds of them listed with low multiples.

There are times when an investor is justified in buying a stock with a high P/E multiple. That is when the earnings of the company are increasing very rapidly and show evidence of continuing to increase substantially in the years ahead. If the rapid growth is expected to continue for years, and it certainly has been predictable for some companies in their early growth stage, then the stock is a buy. This was the case in early 1963, when I was contemplating buying Xerox. At the time the P/E was 39, which was then very high as compared with most other stocks. But the rapid growth features of the stock were so obvious that in this case the high P/E was justified. Subsequently, the stock continued its superperformance price rise and the P/E ratio expanded to as high as 77. The following January the stock was split 5 for 1. So a high P/E ratio should not, by itself, discourage an investor from purchasing a stock; it is only one element among many to be considered.

Recently I came across an old 1958 tabulation of stocks that gave their P/E ratios. IBM had a P/E ratio of 48.7 and was owned by 367 institutions; today 1,131 hold the stock. Many investors at that time probably thought that the P/E was too high and discounted too much future growth. The correct approach for the investor is to determine whether the company will have rapid and consistent growth in earnings. If a company has that, the P/E usually will not be too high, and years later the purchase will be regarded as having been a tremendous bargain. In comparison, duPont E. I. de Nemours had a P/E ratio of 31 in 1958. Many investors evidently preferred duPont to IBM, since duPont stock was owned by 608 institutions, now 367 hold the stock. The performance of the two companies can be compared by referring to Chart 25 for IBM and Chart 26 for duPont.

Higher growth rates justify higher P/E ratios. But it

CHART 25. INTERNATIONAL BUSINESS MACHINES

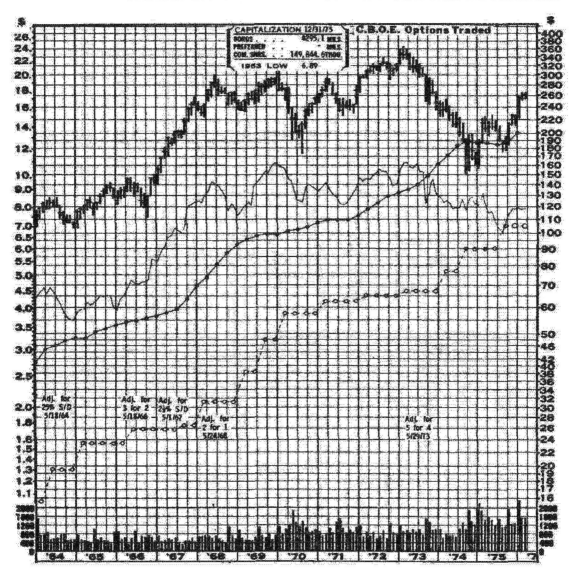

Over the past decade the rise in the price level of IBM common stock has been in concert with increased institutional ownership. The total market value of IBM is over $39 billion.

Chart by Securities Research Company

CHART 26. Du PONT E.I. de NEMOURS

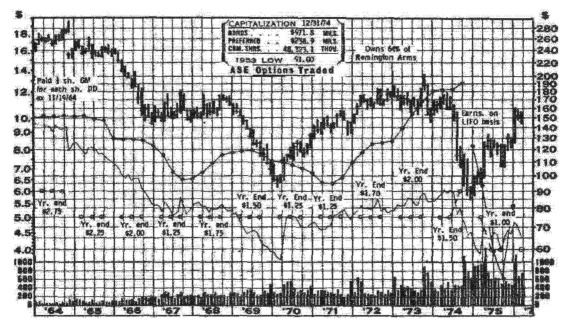

Over the past decade there has been a decrease in the number
of institutions owning Du Pont stock. The decline in the stock's
price reflects this lack of interest by institutions.

Chart by Securities Research Company

is the growth rate expected of the company in the future that justifies the high P/E. Quite often just the opposite occurs, and a stock is given a high P/E after the rapid-growth phase has occurred. And frequently stocks that are about to have rapid growth have low P/E's because the strong future growth potential has not been discovered by investors. For example, Xerox had a much higher P/E in 1967 and 1972, after its growth rate had slowed, than it had in early 1963, when its rapid-growth phase was in an early stage. This same phenomenon occurs repeatedly.

The Ideal Situation

Many stocks have had high P/E's for years, but have had relatively slow rates of growth. It is difficult to justify a P/E of 50 when earnings are increasing at about 5 percent per year. One question to ask yourself before buying a stock with a high P/E ratio is: "Does the rate of increase in earnings justify a P/E ratio at this high level?"

An ideal situation is to find a strong growth stock with a low P/E ratio. It is possible to find such stocks, particularly when virtually the entire stock market is weak and is depressing rapidly growing companies along with the stagnant ones. The big sell-offs of 1962, 1966, 1970, and 1974 created these conditions, and they were ideal times to make stock purchases. Pessimism was dominant and the P/E ratios were relatively low.

Chapter 11
Look for Good Sponsorship

Sponsorship is the recommendation or promotion of a stock with the intent or expectation that it will rise in price. Stockbrokers often sponsor stocks, which they usually recommend widely to their customers and frequently to the public. Companies sometimes sponsor their own stock by making purchases in the open market. This is frequently done for employee pension funds. Widely read investment services also act as sponsors when they make purchase recommendations.

One commonly used type of sponsorship is the investment or market letter. There are hundreds of these reports or letters, most of which are mailed weekly to a list of subscribers, usually with specific stocks being recommended for purchase. Another type of sponsorship includes the recommendations that stockbrokers make to their customers. In the large brokerage firms that have offices nationwide the list of stocks recommended for purchase is drawn up in a central securities research office, usually in New York. Thus, when thousands of investors in dozens of offices are advised that a specific stock is highly recommended, that action constitutes strong sponsorship. A third type of sponsorship is the buying support that a large investor, often an institution or the company itself, gives to a stock when the stock's price declines to a predetermined support level.

The important question to ask yourself when you see a stock being sponsored is: "How good is the sponsorship?" Some sponsorship can be sound, especially that of certain of the large research organizations that expend considerable amounts of money and effort in their analyses of companies. But there are some market letters that can do the investor more harm than good. Evaluate their recommendations carefully. In mid-1968, only weeks before the stock market began a new bear market, I received a considerable number of unsolicited market letters advising the purchase of stocks.

Individual investors should be particularly wary of low-price stock promotions. Back in the 1950s there were hundreds of promotions involving new oil and uranium stocks and, later, electronics stocks. Some of them became successful companies, but most of them eventually disappeared from the scene.

But there is another type of promotion that is much more prevalent. This occurs when an honest and respected analyst researches a stock and makes a buy recommendation without taking into account all of the numerous influences that are described in this book. He might not take into account, for example, changing investor psychology, which might suddenly give a P/E ratio of 15 to a stock that for years had enjoyed a P/E ratio of 30 or more. This has happened to many stocks. Boeing, for instance, in late December 1973 had a P/E ratio of about 9. A year earlier the ratio was over 17, and several years earlier the ratio was at 45 or higher. But the attitude of investors toward the company had changed, and they were not as willing to pay as much for earnings as they once had been. Changing investor psychology is a force that can cause the best of investment advisors to make bad mistakes. It might have very little to do with the financial status of a particular company. It is often concerned principally with the confidence that investors feel regarding the future of the nation and its economy.

Stock promotion is often aimed at capturing the imagination of investors, who are told a story about the big plans of a company. If the promotional campaign is successful, the price of a stock can be run up, sometimes quickly, even though the company might go bankrupt a few years later. If investors have been burned by promotions too often, or if the promotion is not convincing, the stock's price is unlikely to rise.

Several years ago I was busy at my desk when the telephone rang. It was a broker friend who wanted to let me in on a great opportunity to buy some stock in a northeastern brewery. My reaction was: "Where is the great potential in a regional brewery?" I told my friend that I would let him know if I decided to buy. During the next few days I watched the stock's action on the financial pages and noticed that the price had dropped sharply.

"What happened to your beer stock?" I asked a few days later. "I see that it's down about fifteen points."

"Well," my friend replied, "that's quite a story. It seems that the president of the brewery gave that bullish tale to one of our vice-presidents, then unloaded a big block of his own stock. I think we were taken."

A company's management can sponsor its stock in other ways as well; the most common is by issuing favorable quarterly earnings reports, which, unlike the annual reports, are not audited.

Most investors who buy stock being sponsored or promoted are afraid of missing the action, of passing up a budding Xerox or Syntex. The best approach is to avoid jumping in until you have evaluated the stock thoroughly. If it still looks good, your next problem is to determine when to buy it.

An Example of Sponsorship

In early 1974 there was an interesting example, shown on Chart 27, of sponsorship by a company's management. The company, Athlone Industries, is one of the largest manufacturers of stainless-steel plate and a major distributor of industrial fasteners. During the severe sell-off of October-December 1973 Athlone declined to 10. Starting in early January the stock's price climbed steadily, reaching 24 in June 1974. This occurred during a period of general weakness in the stock market, but

Athlone received a considerable amount of favorable publicity during the period. On April 5,1974, the Value Line Investment Survey ranked Athlone highest for probable market performance during the next twelve months. At the time, the stock's price was fourteen dollars, its yield was 6.6 percent, and the P/E ratio was 3. Value Line included Athlone in a new industry group, "Specialty Steels." The evaluation of the Speciality Steels stated that the outlook for stainless steel was more favorable than in many years.

On April 30,1974, Athlone announced that it had repurchased 132,000 of its common shares since the beginning of the year. On May 31 the company announced that it had purchased 25,000 shares of its common stock for $468,750, bringing the company's purchases that year to 157,000 shares. At the annual meeting on May 17 the company chairman estimated 1974 sales at $240,000,000 up from 1973 sales of $187,970,000. He estimated that net income per share might exceed $7.50 and could conceivably double 1973's results.

During the 1974 period the company also placed advertisements in the *Wall Street Journal* and was the subject of a feature story in *Forbes.* Standard & Poor's *Stock Reports* on June 24, 1974, predicted a substantial earnings gain and stated that the shares were appraised conservatively. Stay alert for sponsorship of this kind, where the fundamentals of a company appear to be excellent, where the management is actively supporting the stock, and respected advisory services recommend its purchase or retention.

Sponsorship by Institutional Investors

Purchases by institutional investors can also give strong sponsorship to stocks. The trick is to select stocks that they are buying or will buy, and to avoid stocks that they are selling or will sell. So it is often wise to avoid

CHART 27. ATHLONE INDUSTRIES

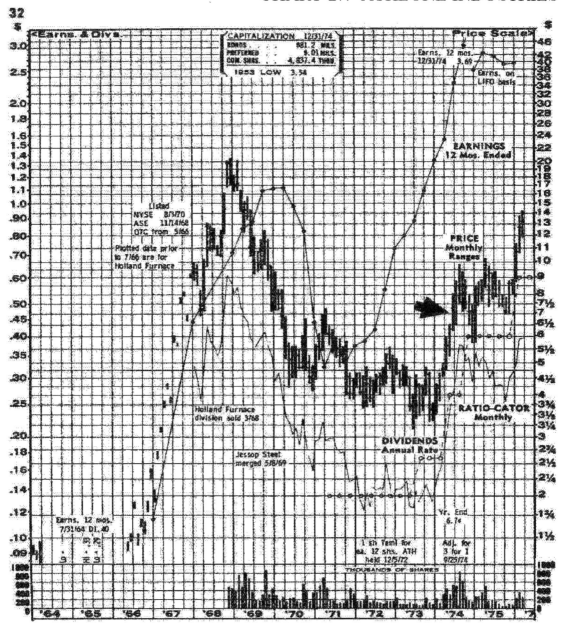

This is an example of an exceptionally strong stock that moved higher, against the downward trend of the vicious 1974 bear market. Most stocks move with the primary trend. Athlone received strong sponsorship early in 1974 and had a very large increase in earnings.

Chart by Securities Research Company

stocks in which hundreds of institutions have held large positions for years. Some of those holdings are probably growing stale and will be sold. In contrast, there are always stocks in which institutions are just beginning to show interest.

Although mutual funds have received much more publicity, their assets are dwarfed by the larger and more numerous corporate and state pension funds. A survey of institutional investments was made by the publication, *Institutional Investor* and printed in the August 1976 issue. The 300 largest institutional funds have total assets exceeding $685 billion, which are managed by bank trust departments, insurance companies, and management companies. There are seventy-eight money managers each managing more than $1 billion worth of stocks. Moreover, the pension funds are constantly growing in size because of employees' payroll contributions. This factor of increasing institutional participation tends to give a bullish long-term bias to the stocks of companies that begin to develop institutional interest.

More than 70 percent of the daily trading volume on the New York Stock Exchange is now made by institutions, which number over two thousand. Over the past ten to fifteen years the extent of their activity has grown phenomenally. Yet their mere size puts them at a disadvantage compared with alert individual investors. The latter can go into a 50, 80, or even 100 percent cash position quickly if there is a market break or an adverse news development indicating an approaching bear market, whereas a $500 million pension fund is not as flexible.

Professional money managers have been wrong at crucial market turning points when the public was right. A 1970 study revealed that in late 1968 and early 1969, near the top of a bull market, institutions were buying while the public was selling. Near the bottom of the subsequent bear market, in May-July 1970, institutions were sellers while odd-lot customers were buyers. An

154

alert and trained nonprofessional who is willing to give the necessary time and attention to managing his investments should be able to do as well as most institutional investors.

Institutions were heavily invested in the Penn Central when the railroad entered bankruptcy in the summer of 1970. There were 99 institutions with 1,608,000 shares in June 1970. Two years earlier, in July 1968, there were 105 institutions that owned 4,061,000 shares. By May 1969 these totals had declined to 102 institutions and 3,231,000 shares, but by January 1970 the number of institutions had increased to 110, although the total shares held declined to 1,925,000. Even in October 1970, after the bankruptcy, there were 89 institutions with 1,022,000 shares. With very large blocks of stock, institutional investors have difficulty getting out of a deteriorating situation even when they want to. Most funds lack the flexibility of the individual investor.

Ten or fifteen years ago the institutions concentrated their holdings in stocks such as duPont, General Electric, General Motors, AT & T, Union Carbide, and U.S. Steel. Today more institutions own McDonald's than U.S. Steel; more own Xerox than duPont; more own Burroughs than Kennecott Copper. Institutional ownership of General Motors, General Electric, and AT & T has declined but is still large. In order to benefit from all of this institutional activity involving billions of dollars, the individual investor should try to figure out where the institutions will be investing their money in the future.

One approach is to determine which stocks the institutions are buying. By comparing the number of institutions holding a stock at specific times it is possible for an individual to determine whether it is being acquired or distributed by institutional managements. It is advisable to select stocks that are beginning to be accumulated by institutions rather than stocks that have been held for many years by hundreds of institutions; in the latter situation distribution of stock is as likely as additional purchases. Back in 1962 there were 575 institutions that owned U.S. Steel common stock; by the end of 1972 the number owning U.S. Steel had declined to 63. The stock's performance during the period is shown in Chart 28. In contrast, Chart 29 is of a stock that has been a favorite of institutional investors during the past decade. At the beginning of 1965, Burroughs stock was in the portfolios of 39 institutions and had a P/E ratio of about 17. At the end of 1973 Burroughs was held by 316 institutions and its P/E ratio was over 40. The Earnings line reveals that the company has had an earnings trend that generally has been consistently rising, a feature that attracts institutional interest.

The institutional holdings of stocks are published on a monthly basis and it is not difficult for an individual investor to determine if institutions are accumulating or distributing the stock of a particular company. It is reassuring to an investor to know that a stock he is about to purchase is being accumulated steadily by institutional investors. During weak markets their strong financial resources have tended to support the stocks in which they are interested.

Xerox, shown on Chart 30, is a stock that has had strong institutional sponsorship for about ten years. In 1964, when Xerox split its stock 5 for 1, there were newspaper stories saying that the action would permit increased institutional participation. It is interesting to see the extent of that participation since then, as shown in the following table. The information was derived from Standard & Poor's monthly *Stock Guide.*

Table 6

Date	Number of Institutions
September 1963	88
January 1964	89
May 1965	125
May 1966	213
November 1966	278
June 1967	314
January 1968	387
July 1968	450
May 1969	437
January 1970	488
March 1970	500
June 1970	504
October 1970	637
August 1972	485
December 1973	579
November 1974	647
December 1975	580
September 1976	575

The various periods listed are not precisely comparable since the number of institutions surveyed varied. In earlier years fewer institutions were surveyed than in more recent periods.

It is more important to determine the trend of institutional investment in a stock than to be concerned with the number of institutions owning it. After a stock has been in a portfolio for a long time and has not performed as well as expected, investment managers, as

CHART 28. U.S. STEEL

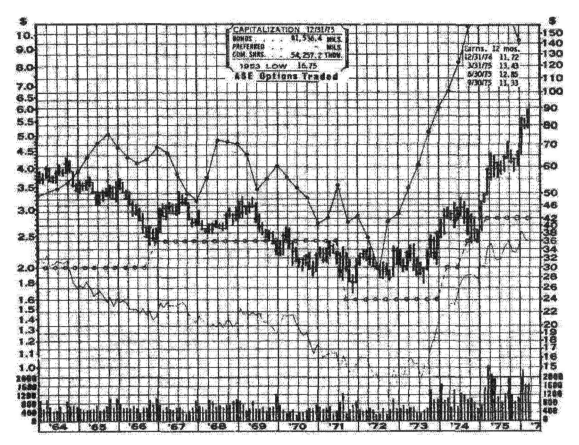

The price of U.S. Steel common stock declined over the past decade along with the number of institutions owning the stock, but in late 1973 and early 1974 institutions were heavy buyers. The rising price trend that began in late 1973 reflects the increased interest in the stock by institutional managements.

Chart by Securities Research Company

CHART 29. BURROUGHS

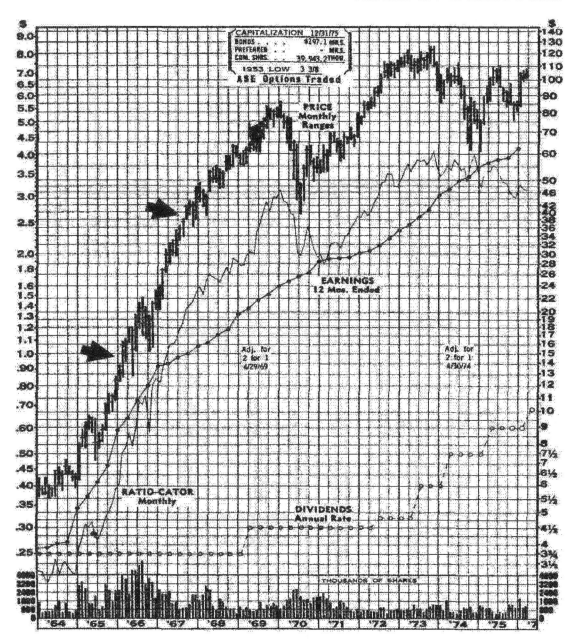

The stock of this major producer of business equipment has been steadily accumulated by institutional investors during the past ten years. The company has had consistently rising earnings since 1964. Arrows indicate superperformance phases.

Chart by Securities Research Company

CHART 30. XEROX

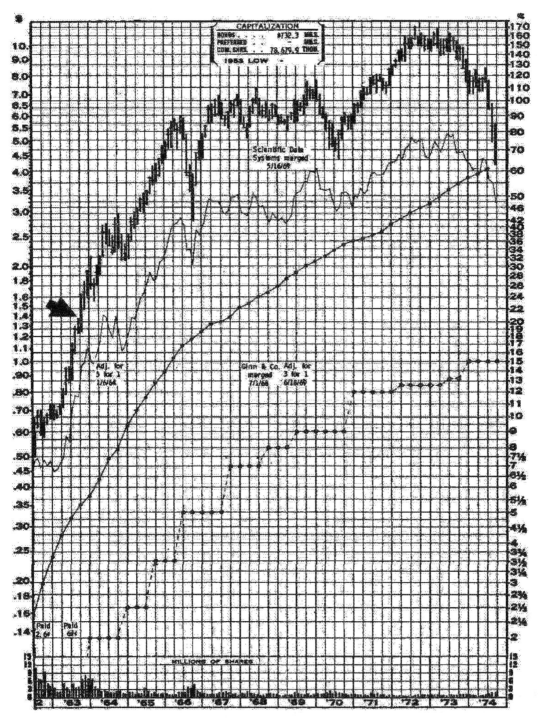

This producer of office copiers is another stock that has been
accumulated heavily by institutional investors over the past
decade. The arrow indicates a superperformance price move.
The rate of growth has been slower since 1966.

Chart by Securities Research Company

well as individual investors, become disillusioned and switch to another investment. The fastest growth of a company, and the most likely time for superperformance of its stock, occurs when the company is relatively small. But many worthwhile gains can also be made in the stock of larger companies if they develop increased institutional sponsorship.

What is the attitude of many institutional managers toward earnings? They look for consistently rising earnings—particularly if the earnings advance enough—and they will pay a high premium if the rate of the rise is steep enough. But they are uninterested in stable, dependable earnings if they are not rising.

Glamour stocks with rising earnings are in demand; mature, stable companies, even of high quality, are neglected. This attitude accounts for the institutional popularity of strong, reliable, and growing companies such as Pfizer, Schlumberger, Kresge, and Schering-Plough. But institutional managers are always looking for something new—tomorrow's glamour stock. It is a challenge to the individual investor to find that stock prior to or at the same time that the institutions discover it.

Trend Following

There are numerous traders in the stock market, many of them very successful, who are convinced that the important thing is to determine if the prices of specific stocks are trending up or trending down and to take a long or short position with the trend. Numerous stock advisory services deal almost exclusively with computer tabulations that show the trend direction and strength of long lists of stocks.

As one more source of evidence to consider before purchasing a stock, technical information of this type can be very helpful in assisting your decision making. It does not make sense for an investor to purchase a stock if its price is in a pronounced downtrend. There is no financial future in fighting the market. Look instead for strong new uptrends.

There are, however, certain problems associated with trends. If you are considering purchasing a stock that is in a price uptrend, you should be concerned with how long the trend will continue. If the uptrend has been in effect for a long period of time there might be a number of stockholders, including performance-minded funds, who are planning to sell. Keep in mind that the sales volume normally peaks out before the price. Following a trend can be very rewarding if you buy the stock early and sell it when the uptrend is broken. Even more rewarding is the ability to anticipate trend changes. Be willing to take profits when a stock's price becomes unrealistically high.

Computerized trend information is of little or no value when stocks are in the process of changing their trends. I have received computer printouts designating stocks as buys on the basis of projected trends on the very day that the stocks have sold off sharply and reversed trend. Moreover, at the best possible buy point—at the very bottom of a bear market—trend studies are of no help. So do not stray from the big strategic picture while engrossed in analyzing technical details.

Spotting Trends

One of the quickest methods of selecting candidates for purchase is to review sets of line charts. Look for stocks that are beginning new uptrends with an increase in the sales volume. Then quickly learn all you can about these stocks. Ask your broker for information. Check reference sources in your library. From your research you should be able to determine almost everything you need to know about each company in order to make an intelligent appraisal. You will learn many details of the company's business, its capitalization, its income statistics for the past ten years, its present and past P/E ratios, the trend of the company's earnings, and the company's near-term and long-term prospects. Perhaps most important, you will have a recommendation or two if the shares appear to have potential long-term appreciation.

It is important to determine the reason for a new uptrend. If it is caused by increased earnings, as many are, the new trend will carry much farther based on, say, a doubling of reported earnings than in cases where the increase was much smaller. To determine what triggered the action it might be necessary to obtain financial newspapers for the day on which the strong new uptrend began. It might also be necessary to enlist the assistance of your broker. When you have determined its cause you will be in a better position to estimate how strong and enduring the new uptrend will be.

Although some stocks remain in strong uptrends for many years, most stock prices are much more erratic in their trends. Stocks often have personalities which are reflected in their long-term charts.

In summary, when you see stocks that are beginning uptrends on a line chart, you should follow up this information by reviewing other material, including the points described in this book, and apply it to that specific stock.

The Sequence of Trend Following

The following sequence of events sometimes occurs when a stock begins a new uptrend. A large purchaser, usually an institution, begins to accumulate the available supplies of stock for sale. Traders and trend followers discover the new activity in the stock and buy to be where the action is. This causes the sales volume to increase and the price to continue rising. Many more trend followers buy with the trend. Shares are being purchased because someone else is buying the stock. The continued rise becomes a phenomenon of mass psychology. Eventually some individualist, probably the fund manager who started the uptrend by buying the stock when it was depressed and unwanted, decides to take profits. He sells a large block. Other institutions, seeing the new weakness and afraid of losing their paper profits, suddenly decide that they prefer cash too. The share price is knocked down and now a downtrend begins. It is therefore important not to be late. Buy when the new rising trend is in an early phase and sell when there is evidence that deterioration is beginning.

When you select a stock only on the basis of its tape action or chart action, you are buying it because someone else thinks it is a good buy. If, on the other hand, the fundamentals of the company also appear to be bullish and if there is an earnings uptrend, an expandable P/E ratio, and a large potential sales growth, then there is probably justification for the stock purchase. But never become a slave of the computer; do not buy simply because the computer says "buy." No one has told the computer about the news developments and trend reversals that lie just ahead. Do not become overly optimistic; stay alert for possible stock distributions and the resulting price reaction.

News, Publicity, and Stock Prices

News and publicity have a strong influence on stock prices, particularly when widely disseminated, as is the case in the United States today with nationwide television network news and nationally distributed magazines and newspapers.

The type of news that often upsets investors is that which makes the future uncertain. Investors are concerned with the future, with anticipated events. Sudden, good, and unanticipated news can trigger wild buying enthusiasm. Bad news, such as the 1962

164

Cuban missile crisis, often causes severe sell-offs.

The constant repetition of news or a particular viewpoint often appears to have greater influence than if the information is printed or broadcast a single time. In 1963, when the newly developed birth control pills were being introduced, the flood of often repetitive stories in newspapers and magazines added tremendously to the fast, volatile run-ups in Syntex and, to a lesser extent, in Searle—the two companies that first introduced the pills. An investor who owns stock in a company that receives favorable widespread publicity is likely to benefit enormously from the quick run-up in the price of the shares.

Sometimes publicity can also lead an investor into a trap, as with the notorious Penn Central case. The railroad stock had received a considerable amount of favorable comment prior to the company's bankruptcy in the summer of 1970. One widely read financial writer for a magazine enthusiastically described in his column the great future for the railroad, then selling at 67 ^{1}/2. He stated that the nonrailroad assets of the $6.5 billion corporation constituted one of the largest real estate enterprises in the world, and he went on to say that the stock offered a most interesting combination of huge assets and excellent management.

Another columnist, writing in a large metropolitan newspaper a few months prior to the railroad's bankruptcy, interviewed a Penn Central director. The columnist quoted the director, who is also a stockbroker, as saying that the Penn Central had the greatest prospects of any stock he knew about, and adding that he did not know of any other stock that could go up in price to five times its present value. He referred to a report on the company by his investment research department that referred to Penn Central's enormous assets per share of $124. The report estimated that the real estate holdings alone were worth in excess of $50 a share, and that transportation investments were probably worth at least $20 to $25 a share.

Publicity, then, favorable and unfavorable, can have a strong influence on the price of any company's stock by persuading investors to buy or to sell. Unfavorable publicity can depress the stock's price; favorable publicity can cause the price to rise. And news and publicity not only play a role in the movement of individual stock prices, but are also very influential in causing the waves of optimism and pessimism that often sweep through large numbers of investors. During the Vietnam war periods of pessimism often alternated with periods of optimism. When the Arab oil embargo was imposed in 1973 the barrage of negative, repetitive news and opinion broadcast by the national television networks and by other news media brought about not only sell-offs in stocks directly affected by the embargo but also declines in stocks with little or no connection to the problem.

On May 27, 1970, at the very bottom of a severe bear market, with the Dow Jones industrials at 627, financial experts on both television and radio were quoted as expecting the averages to decline at least another 100 points. I wondered at the time how many unthinking people acted on the opinions. Similar opinions, predicting additional severe declines, have been expressed on television near the bottoms of other bear markets. Thus, the news networks are instrumental in causing many investors to sell, often shortly before a bear market hits bottom and stocks begin their rebound. Sometimes the reverse is true, of course, and the national news discovers a bull market and gives it publicity just as it is about to top out and start a decline. The best course for an individual investor is to be very wary of financial news on the national television networks and in national news magazines. The result of the barrage of publicity, particularly in promoting bear markets by reiterating the reasons for impending disaster, is that impressionable persons become more and more fearful, so much so that frequently they sell their securities near the bottom of a bear market.

Buy Stocks You Understand

There are some stocks that can be easily understood by most investors, and there are stocks that even highly qualified experts find difficult to understand. The easiest stocks to understand usually belong to companies that are relatively uncomplicated, such as a growing chain of motels or a business with a new product that is well-protected by patents.

Stocks that are difficult to understand, such as most electronics stocks, I tend to avoid. The electronics industry has had tough competition and a history of company failures. However, quite a few years ago I became interested in the stock of a small electronics company that manufactured a variety of components for electronics systems. The stock had very strong sponsorship from a widely read technical market letter and also from a highly respected stock advisory service. I purchased the stock based on their recommendations and on the fact that the stock was in a strong uptrend on a chart. In short, I was buying blindly on the basis of sponsorship and an early uptrend. But the stock always bothered me because I could not figure out the potential market for its products, which were in competition with those of bigger companies. So I sold the stock at a small profit after a few months. Eventually the stock's price went into a decline from which it has not recovered.

When it comes to evaluating high-technology stocks the investor can have a problem. Most of us are not experts in electronics, physics, or engineering. Moreover, estimating the profit potential of new products is often complicated. High P/E ratios and erratic earnings trends are features found in many of these stocks.

Another type of company that is difficult to analyze is the conglomerate. Trying to determine the trends in its various businesses can be very complicated for most investors. There is one conglomerate that is in the following businesses: sulfur production, hearing aids and instruments, boats, natural gas distribution, antipollution devices, and real estate development. How does an individual investor get insight regarding the future of a company like that? I have had some success by noting that the management was trying to raise the price of the company's stock by increasing the earnings per share. This can be accomplished not only by increasing earnings but by decreasing the number of shares outstanding. The reduction is accomplished by techniques such as offering to exchange debentures for common stock, or by having the company purchase its own shares on the open market. Since conglomerates often acquire other companies by exchanging stock, their managements sometimes appear to be strongly motivated to take steps that will increase the price of the common stock.

New information is significant if you have an understanding of the particular company or industry that is affected. But without that understanding you will not see the significance of new facts or developments. In order to see significance in news developments that might relate to specific stocks, it is necessary to understand those stocks. For example, if you own the stock of a company engaged in home construction and you read in the newspaper that the chairman of the Federal Reserve has indicated that the Fed is intent on reining in the nation's expansion of credit, you should be able to see significance in that statement as it relates to your company. So it is important that you buy stocks that you understand.

All investors read the same financial and economic news in newspapers, magazines, and investment advisory services. The difference between individuals is in the way they react to identical information. Some see significance and meaning; others do not.

Part IV
When Should You Sell?

Chapter 12
The Timing Rhythm

At some point a superperformance stock will cease to be a superperformance stock, as Chart 31 of Winnebago Industries dramatically reveals. Even IBM has had price reactions as high as 50 percent. When it appears that a sizable reaction is likely to occur, the prudent approach usually is to sell and then start searching for the next opportunity to buy superperformance at depressed prices.

While safety of investment is derived from the good timing of the purchase, and performance is derived from price volatility, profits and the preservation of capital are derived from the good timing of the sale. And timing the sale is more difficult than timing the purchase because stocks reach their bear market lows simultaneously, but their bull market highs are attained independently. Following the stock averages and selling when the primary trend turns down is often unsatisfactory, since numerous stocks reach their peaks prior to the peaks in the averages. The price and volume trend for each stock must be studied independently and action taken accordingly.

Just as an investor should try to make purchases when a stock is depressed in price, he should attempt to sell after a stock's price has surged. Just as stocks are technically strongest when the price has been depressed for a long time and everyone who might sell has already sold, a stock is technically weakest after prices have risen steadily for a considerable period of time; the number of investors who have paper profits and who are tempted to cash in rises as the stock's price rises.

One of the most effective methods used to determine when to sell a stock is to follow its action on a chart daily. If the price begins to decline and breaks a

CHART 31. WINNEBAGO INDUSTRIES

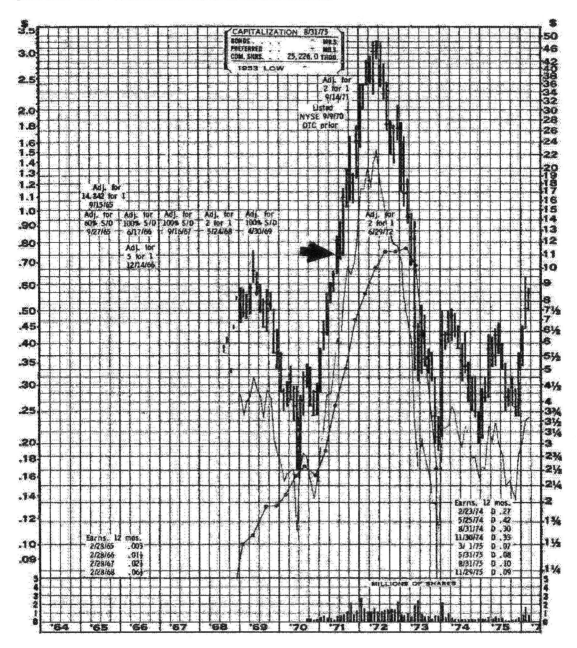

This chart of Winnebago, the country's largest producer of motor homes, shows dramatically that when fortunes of a rapidly growing company change suddenly, the decline in the price of its stock can be extreme.

Chart by Securities Research Company

predetermined "sell" level, call your broker and tell him to sell.

The year-end period—December, January, February—is the time of the year when bull markets most often change to bear markets. Bear markets began in January 1973, January 1960, February 1966, December 1968, and January 1973.

A review of the time spans of superperformance phases might be helpful to an investor who is trying to determine when to sell, or whether to buy a stock that is already in a strong uptrend. Few rapid price increases last longer than two and a half years and many have durations of less than a year. About half of the rapid price increases have durations of twelve to twenty-four months.

The National Economy and Stock Market Declines

It is easier to anticipate general market declines than declines in individual stocks. Stock averages turn down in response to evidence that federal officials are initiating steps to slow down the nation's economy because of inflationary pressures and an excessive use of credit. But even if there were no active government participation in slowing a boom, the expansion phase of the cycle would eventually end and the business decline and contraction would take place. As costs increase, inflation accelerates and consumers begin to resist paying the higher prices.

Money moves the markets. High interest rates reflect the high demand for money. Rising interest rates mean that the yields of new bond issues are higher, so investors purchase them in preference to lower-yield old bonds or stocks purchased for dividend income. The old bonds and the income stocks decline to prices at which they become competitive with the new bonds. A booming economy in which demand for bank credit is soaring is likely to result in money becoming scarce, particularly if the Federal Reserve does not take steps, which are inflationary, to compensate for the increased demand. The cost of money increases and stock prices become depressed as money moves out of stocks and into bonds.

Although the nation's economy is usually strong when presidential elections are held, business contractions often occur near the time of midterm congressional elections. The business contractions that frequently occur approximately midway through a presidential term are probably a principal reason why the political party in control of the White House loses congressional seats in midterm elections. Midterm congressional elections were held in 1946, 1950, 1954, 1958, 1962, 1966, 1970, and 1974. Economic recessions occurred in 1945, 1949, 1953-54, 1957-58, 1960-61, 1970, and 1974-75. In 1966, moreover, there was a period of tight money and declining business which was not labeled an official recession. A comparison of these two lists reveals that there is a close correlation between the years of midterm congressional elections and years in which recessions occurred.

Presidential Elections and the Stock Market

The four-year bull market-bear market pattern cannot be guaranteed to continue in the future, but there is a good, specific reason for believing that it will. The political party that is in control of the White House and the executive branch of the Federal Government is understandably reluctant to lose the office because of voter dissatisfaction with poor economic conditions in the country, such as high unemployment, declining business profits, and falling stock prices. As a result, most recent presidential-election years have been prosperous years and incumbent administrations will try to make them prosperous in the future. But after the election there is less concern for maintaining a high level of prosperity and there is increased determination to fight inflation, so anti-inflation measures are usually taken.

Individual investors should be aware of this government-related cyclical pattern or scenario in order to plan the timing of purchases and sales more effectively. Presidential-election years are likely to witness a strong stock market, but a bear market is likely to begin during the first two years following the presidential election. By anticipating government fiscal and monetary policies you will be able to stay ahead of the technical evidence that most of the experts use as a basis for decisions.

The key factor determining whether or not stock prices will remain strong after a presidential election lies in the results of the election. If investors perceive that a new president is likely to start a new wave of inflation harmful to stock prices, they are likely to react by selling. In fact, stock prices can begin to turn weak even prior to presidential elections if the investing public believes that they know who the winner will be, and know that his policy positions will be detrimental to investment in stocks.

The results of elections sometimes catch investors by surprise, as in 1948 when Harry Truman defeated Thomas E. Dewey. The day after the election, stock prices dropped sharply and continued to decline for months.

A general strategy for timing stock purchases and sales could consist of buying stocks during the bear market between presidential elections and selling stocks around election time. The general strategy should be modified whenever market conditions do not appear to be following this theoretical pattern.

Although investors should plan purchases and sales within a general strategy that takes into account the four-year political and stock-price cycles, they should also be alert and willing to change their strategy if important events or surprises occur. After all, if a major war breaks out, the entire scenario is radically changed.

It is a matter of being in tune with the times, of being aware of the ebb and flow of national interest, money, and effort. Always be ready for the unexpected.

Watch Out for Surprises

Surprises are sudden, unexpected changes. The Cuban missile crisis of 1962 and the Arab oil embargo of 1973 were surprises. No one had advance information. The stock market could not discount the event in advance. The professional has no advantage over the individual investor when a surprise news development occurs. In fact, he is at a decided disadvantage: Most individuals can sell their comparatively small holdings quickly, if necessary, but it is more difficult for a fund manager to dispose of or even reduce his much larger portfolio. Surprises usually trigger a new price trend, so be prepared to take action quickly.

Because of the element of surprise, it can be risky for an investor ever to be excessively bullish or bearish. We live in an age when the Dow Jones industrials frequently move twenty points or more in a day. Volatile stocks often move ten points or more in a single session, and low-priced stocks sometimes gain or lose one-fourth or one-third of their value. Bad news that comes as a surprise results in a sharp stock market sell-off. The surprise war in the Middle East and resulting Arab oil embargo caused a two-hundred-point drop in the Dow Jones industrials in just twenty-eight trading sessions, or in slightly over a month, which was one of the sharpest sell-offs on record. The average loss per day of the Dow Jones industrials was over .7 percent—almost the same rate of decline that occurred in 1929 over sixty-five trading sessions. Individual stocks declined even more sharply. An example of a stock that sold off very sharply on the surprise news is shown on Chart 32, Outboard Marine.

Looking ahead, investors should consider how their

CHART 32. OUTBOARD MARINE

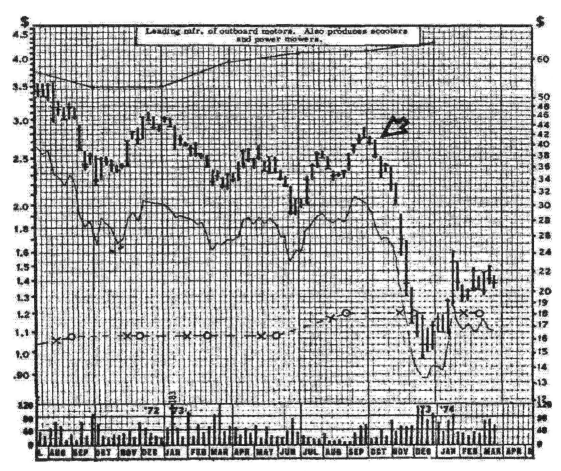

Leading mfr. of outboard motors. Also produces scooters and power mowers.

The surprise energy crisis affected some stocks much more severely than others. Outboard Marine, the nation's largest producer of outboard motors, was especially hard hit by the sudden development in early October 1973.

Chart by Securities Research Company

177

stocks will react if Congress modified tax laws to treat capital gains as regular income. By anticipating possible future events and taking precautionary action before the events occur, the element of surprise is reduced and stock market losses may possibly be minimized or averted.

To Hold or to Sell?

There are some individuals who hold on to their stocks indefinitely. It was estimated recently that many billions of dollars' worth of stocks are held by investors who consider themselves to be locked in because they do not want to pay taxes on their capital gains. In some cases the profits simply disappear.

My review of the price action following the 589 1962-1974 superperformance price moves revealed that only 85 of the price moves ended without a severe price reaction of 10 percent or more, and that 198 of the bull moves were eventually canceled by declines as large as or larger than the superperformance price move.

If he is to be successful in the stock market the individual investor must not be late in carrying out buying and selling decisions. Buying good stocks at the wrong time causes problems for more investors than purchases of hopelessly poor stocks. Likewise, it is obviously a mistake to delay selling in a market that has turned bearish. There are times when it is good policy to sell a stock simply because it has stopped going up. But this decision has to be made by studying the specific stock, its price and earnings history, its potential, and numerous other factors. Once the decision has been made to sell, do not delay. The bottom can sometimes be a long way down, as is revealed by some of the charts in this book. Some stocks never come back, and for those that do return to former price levels, the waiting period can sometimes be long.

Often investors continue to hold a stock after it has

had a substantial run-up in price. Sometimes it is helpful in determining whether you should continue holding a stock to ask yourself if you would be willing to buy the stock now, after the price run-up. If the answer is no, why expect someone else to buy it? A stock that shows signs of deterioration or appears to be overpriced should be sold.

When purchasing a stock investors usually consider the risk involved versus the profit potential, often referred to as the risk/reward ratio. But after they have owned a stock for a few years, many investors cease evaluating it. Usually this is the time that the risk of potential loss should be considered, for the reasons justifying the stock's purchase may no longer be valid.

Be Alert to Federal Policy Switches

Just as the Federal Reserve System can encourage the stock market by loosening credit and stimulating spending in the national economy, the Federal Reserve can also depress bull markets by restricting the supply of credit, inhibiting spending. Not all bull markets end because of U.S. Government monetary and fiscal policies, however. Prices in the 1961 bull market apparently reached such high levels that they could not go any higher, because the prices of many stocks were discounting developments too many years in the future. When they reach price levels that are unrelated to tangibles such as earnings, prices fall even if there is no depressing influence such as a threatened recession. Evidently there are enough investors who, realizing that prices are out of line compared with traditional values, decide to take profits. The market in general is too high when adverse news triggers a psychological reaction that results in high-volume selling. If bad news occurs when the market is relatively low, the reaction is usually not as severe. In other words, the stock market is too high when investors perceive it to be too high, and the market is not too high if investors do not panic from bad news. The market action itself determines whether a particular stock or the market in general is too high. And this should usually determine whether you should sell or hold a position.

Since stock market movements are a result of a complex mixture of mass psychology, world and national politics, economic policies, and buying power, it is vital that you stay alert to changes in these forces and be ready to sell positions quickly if necessary. Any sharp decline in the stock market should be regarded as a warning. If your stock has had a sharp run-up and shows as a spear formation on a line chart, you should give serious consideration to selling or to establishing stop-loss positions. The chart of Winnebago Industries, Chart 31, shows an example of a stilt pattern in the price of that stock, resulting from a strong sell-off following a period of rapid price appreciation.

It graphically illustrates why it is necessary to sell some stocks quickly when they start to plunge after a strong superperformance bull move. When a stock's price begins to plunge it is very difficult to determine at what level the drop will stop, because most selling on the way down develops a strong panicky, emotional character. Margin calls accelerate and extend the slide. It is better to take profits early and then start looking for the bottom of the decline and new buying opportunities.

Even well-established blue chip growth stocks have periods of weakness that can cause sharp reactions in their price. A recent example is the decline in Avon Products, shown on Chart 33, from a high of $139^3/4$ in early 1973 to under 25 in 1974. Stocks with very high P/E ratios can often be susceptible to sharp declines when the primary market trend turns down.

A Possible Exception

There is one type of stock that sometimes might better be held rather than sold and repurchased. This is the

180

CHART 33. AVON PRODUCTS

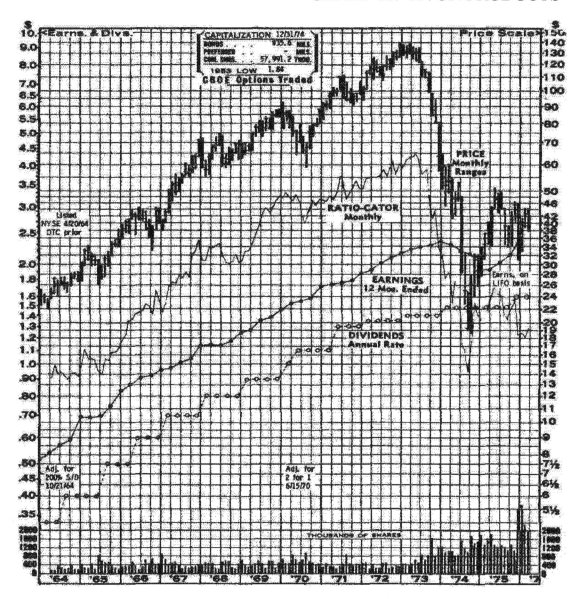

Stocks of the strongest growth companies sometimes should
be sold if the stock becomes extremely overpriced or if conditions
within the company indicate a slower rate of growth. Sometimes
the stock becomes radically oversold and becomes a good buy
again. Avon Products is the world's largest manufacturer of
cosmetics and toiletries, specializing in house-to-house sales.
Chart by Securities Research Company

181

stock of a budding growth company that has not had a price run-up. Typically, it might be a small company that is beginning to market a unique new product but whose stock price has not increased substantially. Examples are Xerox and Syntex when they were in their very early stages and had not started to benefit, in terms of stock price, from their vast growth potential.

The Pricing Rhythm

Not only is there a timing rhythm to stock prices, but also a pricing rhythm. Stock prices move through stages, as can be readily seen on some of the charts in this book. The sequence of action consists of, first, the establishment of a base, formed sometimes over a period of years. Gradually the price begins to rise, then accelerates into an upswing stage with the price consistently advancing. The upswing stage is gradually replaced by a stage during which the price stops advancing, but moves irregularly sideways. This stage is the top, and professionals often refer to a stock as looking "toppy." Stocks in this stage of price movement should be sold, for the fourth and last stage is the downtrend. The declines in many stocks retrace their entire advancing stage, as was indicated in Chapter 7. Eventually the price of the stock declines to a new base, and it might remain at that level for years.

The stages of base, upswing, top, and decline often result from patterns of accumulation and distribution by professionals, who accumulate stock when it is in a base and sell when the price has advanced. Their buying activity often triggers interest in the stock by technical analysts and investors, who watch computer printouts and charts to learn what "big money" is doing. After a price advance has occurred and the public has become interested in the stock, the professionals begin to sell, or "distribute." The price ceases to advance, but trading volume can be heavy. The third stage, the "top," has been reached. The professionals have sold their stock and there is no longer any motive for supporting the market. As the price starts to decline the public begins to sell, accelerating the decline. Eventually the price reaches a new base, at which level the process of accumulation begins again.

It is therefore desirable to buy stock just as an upswing is beginning and to sell after the price has stopped advancing. It is very important not to be late buying and not to be late selling. In this Wall Street version of musical chairs anyone who is caught owning stock when the music stops is a dunce.

A Big Problem for Investors: The Stock Exchange Specialists

Defenders of the use of specialists by the exchanges contend that they support stocks from declines. This argument is obviously phony. Where was the support in 1974 during the biggest price decline since 1929? Where was their support of Avon Products, which dropped from 140 to under 20? Where did the specialists support Polaroid—at 14 Vs after it had plunged from 143 $^{1}/4$? Specialists and stock exchange insiders are more likely to be the cause of sharp declines. Most investors would be better off without help from the friendly stock exchange specialist. They would prefer to keep their shares of those big trading profits in their own pockets.

An ideal time for individual investors to sell stock is therefore before the stock exchange insiders begin to knock prices down with their heavy short selling. But the advantage is all with the exchange specialist and his buddies on the trading floor. Their books of buy and sell orders tell them the magnitude of the buying and selling pressures, so they know precisely when to begin selling short. The individual investor does not have this advantage. But after a stock has had a sharp price run-up, a protective stop-loss order can be entered a few points lower. If the stock is bombed by large-block short Sailing the position- will be sold automatically.

How Specialists Operate

Since stock exchange specialists and insiders have a very important influence on the direction of stock prices, it might be helpful to analyze the actions that they should take in order to maximize their own profits. Near the bottom of a bear market they accumulate stock in preparation for the approaching rising market. As stock prices rise the insiders are sellers, taking profits on positions they had accumulated at lower prices. As prices continue to rise they become short sellers, having distributed their supply. Their self-interest then dictates lower prices, which are brought about by timely short selling to drive prices down.

The actions of the exchange specialists illustrate a technique that individual investors should learn—that is, to buy stocks when they are quiet, inactive, and depressed, and to sell stocks when the demand for them is strong and prices are surging on high volume. The precise time to sell is when the price and volume surge is ending.

Movements involving price run-ups and shakeouts following heavy short selling are price cycles of short-term or intermediate-term duration that occur within the longer-term four-year cycles brought about by presidential, congressional, or Federal Reserve Board policies related to the four-year political cycle.

Declines in stock prices do not always occur because stockholders have decided to sell. Often the price decline results from short selling by hedge funds, stock exchange specialists, or other big traders. The 1973 Securities and Exchange Commission complaint against Avis revealed that one hedge fund had sold short 25,400 shares of Avis stock, and that the short seller had been given access to information that had not been disclosed to the public. When a speculator sells stock short, he sells borrowed stock and assumes that prices will decline so that the borrowed stock can be covered later by purchasing the shares at a lower price. The price of Avis shares declined from $33.50 on May 16 to under $21 dollars on June 6, 1973, when Avis confirmed the profits from vehicle sales in the company's earnings.

When there are negative news developments or other evidence that a stock should be sold, the public stockholders are often much slower in learning of the developments and in taking action than are the professional traders who stay close to the action on the stock exchange floor. When there is a surprise development indicating that stocks or a stock should be sold, the traders usually manage to sell short or dispose of their holdings before the public has that opportunity.

Do Call Options Depress Stock Prices?

Call options on about 150 stocks are sold on the Chicago Board Options Exchange, the American Stock Exchange, the Pacific Exchange, and the Philadelphia Exchange. A call option is a right permitting the buyer to purchase a stated number of shares of stock at a specific price within a limited time period, usually up to six months. The big disadvantage of such an option is the limited time period in which it can be exercised.

Since it is the public that buys options, hoping for a price rise, the sellers are usually professionals. It is not in the interest of professionals to permit a rise in the price of the stock, so stocks with options are probably depressed in price more than they would be if call options were not traded against them.

Remember the Political Cycle

Individual investors dance to tunes played by Wall Street insiders and big institutional investors. But the music is arranged in Washington. There will continue to be political cycles and business cycles. As a result, there will continue to be widely—and wildly—swinging stock prices as Wall Street insiders try to grab large profits and the public sells in an emotional panic or buys in an emotional euphoria. And in the widely swinging stock markets there will always be superperformance stocks.

A new primary bear market is most likely to start during the period of about fifteen months from the date of presidential elections through the entire first postelection year until the following February. Every primary bear market of the past fifty years, except 1960, has started during that fifteen-month period. If the nation's economy is undergoing a severe inflationary boom when the election is held, measures will be taken to slow the boom and to reduce inflation within a few months following the election; this occurred following the presidential elections of 1937, 1952, 1956, 1968, and 1972. But if the economy is not overinflated, the restrictive policies might be delayed for as much as a year. Following the 1964 presidential election, restrictive actions were not taken until late 1965, about a year afterward.

From the point of view of an incumbent president who wants the nation's economy to be booming at the time of his campaign for re-election, a bear market in stocks and a recession might occur too soon if restrictive monetary policies are taken immediately after his election. For if the bear market and recession begin and end too soon, it would mean that the next bull market in stocks and a booming economy would also occur too soon and they might start another decline before the next election. This is exactly what happened between 1956 and 1960.

Presidential-election year 1956 was a boom year with a strong economy and rising prices. But after the election President Eisenhower expressed fear about the rate of inflation. The Federal Reserve Board began a policy to restrict credit. The result was the 1957-58 recession. Employment reached a peak in mid-1957 and began to decline sharply.

But the stock market turned strong in early 1958, during the depths of the recession, and remained strong for the rest of that year and through 1959. The economy also turned strong. By the time presidential-election year 1960 arrived, however, the economy and stock market had started to decline again, an undesirable prospect from the point of view of an incumbent political party.

A similar pattern happened in 1968, as President Johnson and his economic advisers desperately tried to keep the nation's economy booming until election day that year. But shortly after the election he advocated slowing down the economy because of the threat of accelerating inflation.

Declines in Individual Stocks vs. Declines in the Stock Market

Stocks decline for a variety of reasons related to each specific company and its future prospects. Sometimes earnings are expected to decline and sometimes the stock is simply overpriced.

The stock market, on the other hand, as represented by market averages that include many companies, declines most often because of Federal Government policies such as increasing income taxes, which causes company profits to decline. But the government policy most often used has been to increase the cost of credit and decrease its availability, which is effective in slowing down business activity. Other reasons for declines include the overpricing of numerous stocks, as in late 1961 and late 1968, and widespread investor pessimism, as during the period between 1946 and 1949.

Declines can also be triggered by heavy short selling. This has occurred most often, however, prior to intermediate declines within a primary bull market, as professionals try to drive prices down to levels at which they can cover short sales and re-establish long positions. They are successful because many stockholders are frightened into believing that the price of their stock will decline even further, and therefore decide to sell.

Bear markets can also occur because of the collapse of a pyramid of credit, as happened in 1929. Today's regulations covering credit for stock purchases should prevent widespread forced selling as occurred in that debacle.

Watch for the Warning Signals

The main warning signals for an individual investor to look for, therefore, are the signs of a government-induced slowdown in business activity, which would affect company profits and stock prices.

To find the warning signals it is important to follow the financial news closely, paying particular attention to statements from Federal Reserve Board members and from Administration leaders and economists. But it is also necessary to anticipate economic and political conditions several months ahead. If inflation is becoming a bigger problem, expect that steps will be taken to slow it.

Two key indicators to watch for sell signals are the discount rate, which is set by the Federal Reserve Board, and the interest-sensitive utilities averages. Changes in the discount rate often signal the Fed's intentions to expand or contract the money supply. A rising utilities average is favorable, but be cautious if it has turned down. A comparison of the Dow Jones utility and industrial averages reveals that the utility average began to decline before the industrial average in four of the last six bear markets.

Successful stock market investments are more likely to result from the use of a logical strategy for buying and selling than from a random approach or from the "one decision" method that has been widely accepted by many institutional investors and individuals. The one-decision approach ignores the extreme price volatility that occurs regularly as stock prices move in waves of strength and weakness. The one-decision purchase of Polaroid by institutional investors might have appeared sound in 1971 or 1972, when the stock was selling above $140 a share, but the weakness of the approach was apparent when Polaroid declined to under 20 in 1974. There have been hundreds of similar cases.

To be successful it is necessary to buy the right stock at the right time and to sell it at the right time. You should think like a speculator, but instead of buying today and selling next week, think of buying and selling in terms of the four-year cycles in stock prices. Plan to sell stocks during presidential-election years, when there is very likely to be a strong stock market based on a prosperous economy resulting from expansionist federal fiscal and monetary policies. Plan to purchase stocks close to the bottom of the bear market that occurs regularly during the period between presidential elections. To do this you must follow financial developments very closely in order to determine when the Federal Reserve Board has changed from a policy of monetary firmness to a policy of monetary ease. Moreover, you must be aware of the shift in the psychological attitude of investors from extreme pessimism to optimism.

Investors who are fully invested must sell stock and take profits in order to have sufficient funds available to buy attractive situations after the next sell-off. This is the way fortunes are made in the stock market. You must sell stocks when prices are high in order to have the money to buy attractive stocks when their prices are way down. So do not overstay a bull market. Knowing when to sell your stocks is one of the secrets of success. Regardless of what you, the individual investor, wish to do, stock prices will continue to have bear cycles and bull cycles reflecting business conditions and anticipated business conditions, tight money and plentiful money, increasing earnings and decreasing earnings, booms and recessions. For survival, anticipate. Always stay one jump ahead.

Chapter 13
Selling Short

I recall the evening of the 1968 presidential election, when Richard Nixon defeated Hubert Humphrey in a close vote, not so much because of the details of the election but because of my own activities that evening. As the election returns were being reported, I was seated at a table studying stock charts and company fundamentals. The result of my research was a long list of stocks that I considered to be candidates for short sales. This was the time, I had decided, to sell stocks, without regard to which politician won the election.

The year 1968 experienced a wave of fear-of-inflation psychology. Stock market letters advised readers to "buy stocks now before it is too late." Many stocks were extremely overpriced, but I was convinced that they were also about to be deflated. They were. A few weeks after the 1968 presidential election the Federal Reserve Board adopted policies of increased monetary restraint. The stock market averages reached their peaks in December and the long descent began to the May 1970 bear market lows.

Profits in the stock market can usually be made faster by selling stocks short than by buying them. The reason is that price declines are usually much steeper than price rises, which occur more gradually, over a longer period of time, and are usually accompanied by a healthy amount of pessimism that gradually lessens the longer the price rise continues. Price declines, on the other hand, contain an element of panic that increases as stock prices plunge lower.

A short sale is the sale of borrowed stock, which is arranged for a customer through his stockbroker. A profit or loss is realized when the short sale is covered by a purchase. The short interest—the number of shares that have been sold short and not covered by purchases—is published for New York and American Stock Exchange stocks about the twentieth of each month. The figures are listed in the *Wall Street Journal, The New York Times, Barren's,* and other newspapers.

"Bulls" in the stock market are many times more numerous than "bears." Comparatively few people sell stock short when they expect a decline in prices. A high percentage of short selling is done by the stock exchange specialists on the trading floor. Yet during about one and a half years of each price cycle the primary trend of the stock market is down. In recent years the opportunities for making money fast by selling short in bear markets have been more numerous than the opportunities for rapid capital appreciation in bull markets. During the bear markets that reached their climaxes in 1970 and 1974 there were thousands of stocks which declined to a fraction of their former levels.

One reason for the much smaller number of short sellers is that comparatively little information or assistance is available on the subject. Brokers are oriented toward furnishing information and recommendations for buying stocks, not for selling or short selling.

Timing a Short Sale

The timing of the short sale is of crucial importance. If a stock with a highly volatile price history is sold short at the wrong time, the result could be some quick and sizable losses. Therefore, ask yourself certain questions before you venture to sell a stock short. The questions should include: What stage are we in of the political, business, and stock-price cycles? Are we near the top of a bull market? Which stocks are leading candidates for short sales when prices start to decline? It is important to recognize the end of a bull market and the beginning of a bear market because it is during that transition period that the best opportunities occur for profitable short selling.

The time to sell short is not necessarily identical with the time to take profits in long positions. Stocks do: not all reach their final bull market tops at the same time. Moreover, the stock market averages usually form a top which on charts is shown as a broad, trendless pattern often lasting for months, in contrast with stock market bottoms, which are sharp "V" patterns.

In addition, stocks selected for short selling are not likely to be the same stocks that were owned when market prices were rising. Therefore, the action sequence is likely to be to sell stocks that have been owned, wait for the market's primary trend to turn down, then select candidates for short sales. When an investor sells a stock that he has owned for a couple of years and in which he has a sizable profit, he should try to sell out at a price near the top, but the exact highs are much more difficult to predict than are the exact lows at the bottom of a bear market. Usually the most that can be expected is to be able to sell the stock in its high range during the last phase of the bull market.

The safest time to establish short sales, on the other hand, is after stock prices have started to decline and investor psychology is beginning to change from bullish to bearish.

The Ideal Time to Sell Short

How would the stock market be acting when conditions are ideal for selling short? Under ideal short-selling conditions the Dow Jones industrial averages would be starting to decline after making new highs. Fewer individual stocks would be making new highs. During the bull market that peaked in January 1973 for the stock averages, numerous stocks started price declines earlier. Some examples shown in this book are Skyline (Chart 9), Holiday Inns (Chart 14), and Winnebago (Chart 31).

High P/E ratios, over 50 to 1, in many glamour or "growth" stocks are found when conditions are ideal for short selling. In January 1972 MGIC Investment had a P/E ratio of 80 to 1 and the stock sold as high as 95 ^{7}/s. By late 1974 it had declined as low as 6 Vs. The stock is shown in Chart 34.

There is an abundance of evidence, some fundamental and some technical, that reveals the conditions desirable before selling short. Under ideal conditions for short sales the national economy would be booming, but there would be signs that the boom is growing old. Business investment would be at such a high level that it could not be sustained. Interest rates would be in a rising trend. Wage rates would be rising and profit margins declining. Unemployment would be low, but the rate of inflation would be increasing and would be of greater concern to Washington officials. A presidential election would have been held recently. Two periods with these conditions present were late 1968 and 1972, both presidential-election years.

Patterns of Boom and Bust in Real Estate

The real estate market also booms during these periods of widespread national prosperity. In December 1972 Florida was experiencing a large-scale boom in condominiums, one of the largest real estate construction periods of all times. At that time I stopped to inspect a building overlooking the ocean in southern Florida. It was about half completed, but three-fourths of the apartments had been sold, and I was told that prices were to be raised by five thousand dollars on January 1 and another five thousand dollars on March 1. At another condominium under construction buyers were standing in line, checkbooks and pens in hand. But within six months "tight money" had arrived. By the fall of 1973 it was almost impossible to obtain a mortgage loan and sales had declined to a tiny fraction

CHART 34. MGIC INVESTMENT

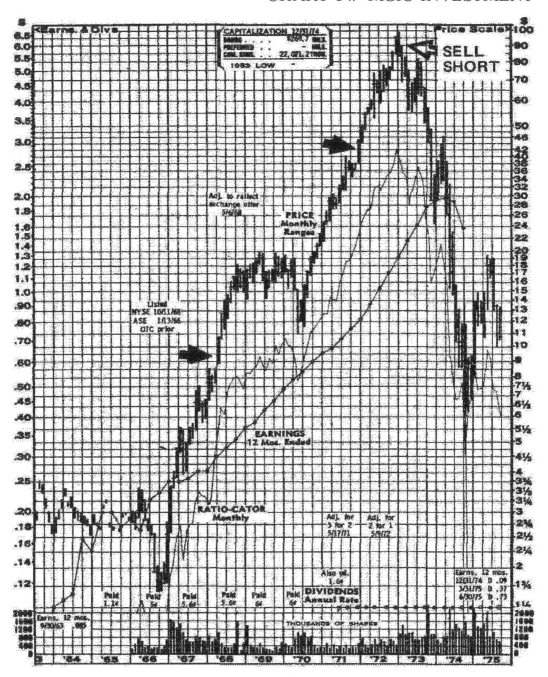

MGIC Investment is the largest private insurer of residential mortgages. The stock had a P/E ratio of 80 to 1 when the stock's price began its decline in January 1973, the same month that the stock market averages began their declines. MGIC's decline accelerated in early 1974, when lower earnings began to be reported.

Chart by Securities Research Company

of the earlier level. By 1974 it was estimated that there were at least ninety thousand empty unsold condominium apartments in Florida alone, and bankruptcies were becoming widespread. So there appears to be a real estate cycle that follows fairly closely the cycles in stock prices. A major factor in slowing down both real estate booms and stock price spirals is, of course, the cost and availability of money.

Profitable Short-Sale Opportunities Have Been Numerous

I reviewed long-term charts to determine how many stocks would have been successful short sales if the short sales had been made in January 1972, when the stock market averages reached their highs and began their slide into the 1973-74 bear market.

Of 1,018 stocks reviewed, 378 would have been unsatisfactory selections. Twenty-eight of these began their declines later than the averages, and the short sale would not have been successful if established in January 1973. The remaining 350 stocks were unsatisfactory for various reasons, including the fact that many of them rallied sharply, late in 1973, before resuming their decline. Others declined, but the extent of the decline was too small to risk a short sale. In other cases stocks did not decline at all, but moved upward against the primary trend of the market, or moved in a sideways pattern.

But there were 640 stocks on which a short sale would have been successful if made at the time the averages peaked. Of these, there were 118 stocks that began their declines at the same time as the averages; 111 stocks had started their declines within the six months prior to the peak in the averages; and the remaining 411 stocks had been declining for more than six months prior to the peaking out of the averages. In most cases their declines accelerated rapidly after the stock averages turned down.

The best candidates for short sales, then, are stocks that have already started to decline when the primary trend of the market begins its downturn. Weak stocks become even weaker when the stock market turns down. An example of this is shown in Chart 35 of Grolier. In this case the stock's price had started to decline before the market averages began their downward movement. The earnings of the company had also started to decline, which is another important factor to look for in selecting a candidate for a short sale. In cases of companies with very high P/E ratios, a reduction in the rate of earnings increase is often sufficient to cause a price reaction.

Rite Aid, shown in Chart 36, and MGIC Investment, shown in Chart 34, are two stocks that began their price slides when the stock market averages began to decline. Both stocks had very high P/E ratios at the time. Their price declines accelerated when their earnings began to decline.

Stocks with high P/E ratios can sometimes be good candidates for short sales, but they are often strong popular stocks and frequently have considerable sponsorship from institutions. So a general conclusion cannot be made that high P/E stocks are usually good short-sale possibilities. The selection has to be based upon other factors, such as the stock's earnings trend and the primary trend of the market, with the P/E ratio just one more factor to be considered. High P/E ratios can quickly call an investor's attention to a stock, however.

Select Short Sales Systematically

Many of the factors that are reviewed in selecting stocks for purchase are also involved in selecting candidates for short sales. Leverage, for example, can work to enlarge a decline in a company's earnings in some years just as effectively as it can enlarge an earnings gain in other years. The heavily leveraged airlines, such as Eastern in

CHART 35. GROLIER

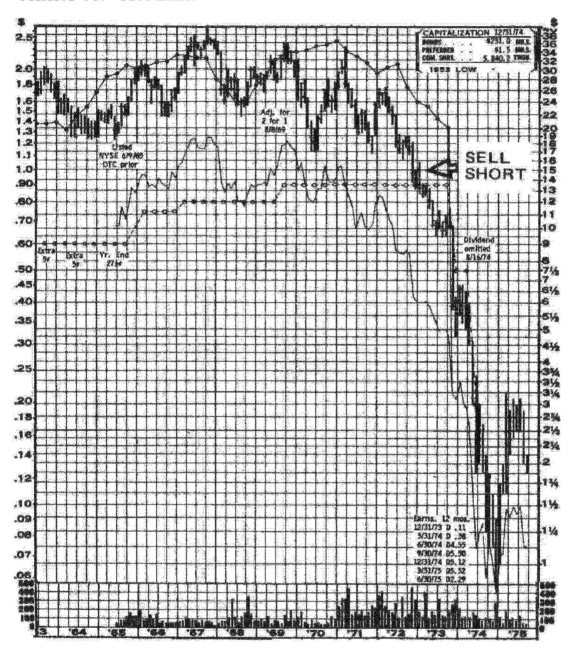

Grolier is a big publisher of reference books, including
Encyclopedia Americana and *New Book of Knowledge*. The
earnings trend and the stock price of this stock were already
declining when the stock market averages began their decline
in January 1973.

Chart by Securities Research Company

198

CHART 36. RITE AID

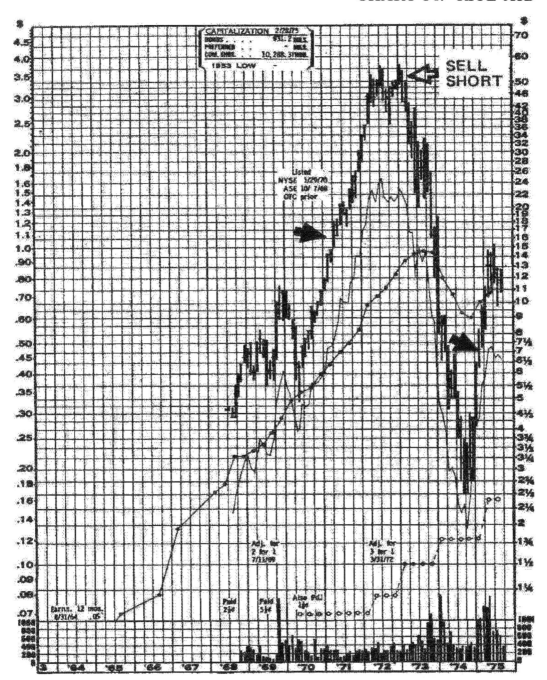

Rite Aid operates discount drugstores in the northeast and is also a food wholesaler. The company's stock began to decline during the same month as the stock market averages, January 1973, but the stock's price decline accelerated after earnings began to decline later that year. The stock had a P/E ratio of 60 to 1 in January 1973.

Chart by Securities Research Company

Chart 37, are an example. Heavy selling by institutions can also cause sharp price declines, just as their heavy buying can cause prices to increase rapidly.

The psychological mood of the investment community and the general news background are important in creating the bear market conditions that are so helpful for successful short selling. The Arab oil embargo that went into effect in late 1973 is one example of the kind of news that creates the widespread pessimism so helpful to short sellers. The repetitious reporting by the news media of rising unemployment figures, of increasing rates of inflation, of rising interest rates, and of war threats are important in overcoming the natural optimism of the American investor.

There are certain stocks that should be avoided, such as those that have large short-interest positions. During bear market rallies these stocks can severely whipsaw a short seller because there are numerous other short sellers who are frantically trying to cover their short sales. Numerous weak stocks that do not have large short positions are more satisfactory from the short seller's point of view because they are much less susceptible to explosive bear market rallies. For similar reasons avoid stocks with very small capitalizations. Select an actively traded stock. It is important to be able to cover the short sale with a purchase without difficulty. When stocks with a history of volatile price moves are sold short, the use of stop orders is sometimes desirable. Buy-stops can be placed about a point above the peak of the last rally.

Short Selling by Professionals

Most short selling is done by professionals—members of the stock exchanges, including specialists. Their activity is published weekly in the "Market Laboratory" section of *Barren's*. But it would be a mistake for individual investors to imitate the short-selling pattern of these insiders. The

200

CHART 37. EASTERN AIRLINES

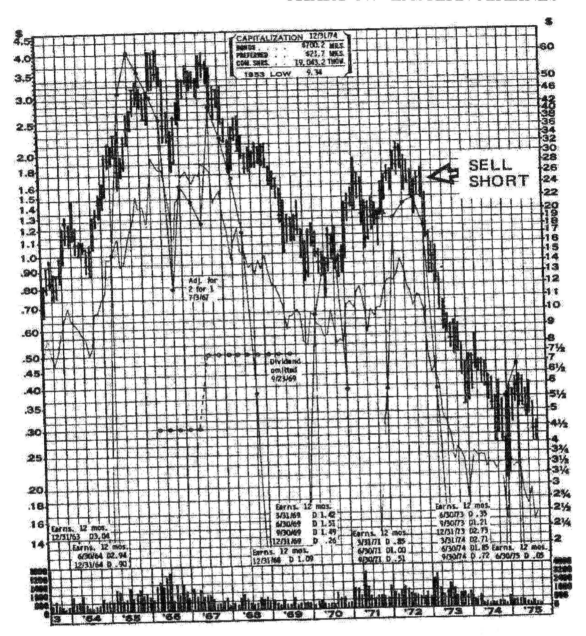

Eastern is one of the largest domestic airlines, operating
primarily along the eastern seaboard. Like most airlines,
Eastern is highly leveraged with debt because of the high cost
of modern jet aircraft. The result is that earnings can fluctuate
wildly from year to year, often having a depressing effect on
the stock's price. Eastern's stock price was already declining
in January 1973 when the market averages began their declines.

Chart by Securities Research Company

201

reason is that much short selling by stock exchange specialists is associated with their market-making activities. They "lean against" the direction of the market. They often sell short heavily when the market averages are rising rapidly. On the occasions when individual investors should be selling short—that is, as prices begin major declines—short sales totals by specialists and insiders have been lower than during market rallies.

One of the heaviest periods of short selling occurred in late 1974, when the stock market averages and most stocks were severely depressed. A severe sell-off occurred in mid-1974, which reached a selling climax on October 4. Stock prices rebounded strongly from the selling climax and regained 100 points on the Dow Jones industrial average within two weeks. It was during this period of strongly rebounding prices that short selling by stock exchange members and specialists was exceptionally heavy.

During the week ending October 11, 1974, for example, total short selling reached 12,105,900 shares, a very high level. Of that total, 8,651,800 shares were sold short by stock exchange members, and of that number 5,432,700 short sales were by stock specialists. The heavy short selling continued for several weeks. The figures for the week ending October 18, 1974, were 9,769,300 shares sold short, of which 7,001,300 were by exchange members—4,510,300 of these by stock specialists. For the week ending October 25, total short sales were 7,317,500, of which 5,147,400 were by stock exchange members; of this number, 3,176,400 were by specialists. Heavy short selling continued during the week ending November 1, 1974. Short sales totaled 8,178,000 shares, of which 5,926,800 were by exchange members and 3,706,300 of that total were by specialists.

The heavy short selling was effective, and reversed the direction of the market. During the week ending November 8, 1974, the Dow Jones industrials dropped 40 points and by the end of the first week in December the decline was more than 170 points. From that level the market began again to rally, as the 1975-76 bull market started to gain strength.

The heavy short selling of October and early November 1974 occurred when stock prices were rising, which is typical of most short selling by professionals. At bull market tops the volume of short selling by stock specialists and other stock exchange members has been somewhat lower. For the week ending December 6, 1968, which was the week when a bull market reached a peak and began the bear market that ended in May 1970, short sales by exchange members totaled 3,219,500 shares, a relatively moderate level of short selling.

The next bull market top for the Dow Jones industrials occurred on January 11, 1973. The volumes of short selling for the week ending January 12, 1973, totaled 5,496,600 shares, of which 4,691,500 were by exchange members; of this latter figure 3,187,800 were by specialists. For comparison, a year earlier, when stock prices were rising sharply from the November 1971 intermediate low of 790.6 on the Dow Jones industrial average, the week ending December 3, 1971, had these figures: total short sales 8,571,700; short sales by exchange members 7,000,100; of the latter total, 5,148,600 were by specialists.

From late November 1971 the market averages climbed steeply for five months. The Dow Jones industrial average rose more than 170 points during the period. Anyone who sold short during the late November-early December 1971 period could have been hurt financially. Heavy short selling by stock specialists, then, is more often associated with rising prices, and it can be unwise for individual investors to do as the specialists do. A safer time for short sales is when stock prices have started major declines.

Covering Short Sales

The best way to select short-sale candidates is by studying long-term charts for direction of price movements,

P/E ratios, and earnings trends. Select stocks that are already declining. As with stock purchases, safety is found in the good timing of the short sale.

When should the short sale be covered? For maximum profits do not cover the short sale until the bear market has run its full course. During the 1969-70 bear market short sales would have been made when the market's primary trend, as revealed by the stock averages, turned down in December 1968; the short sale would have been covered in May 1970 at the bottom of the bear market. Again, in January 1973 the stock market averages began their cyclical decline and short sales would have been made. The covering purchases would have been made during the panic stage of the bear market in October 1974. So short sales should be covered during periods with economic conditions similar to those of May 1970 and October 1974.

The most important economic news of those periods was that Washington political leaders were taking steps to stimulate the national economy. Their moves included increased government spending, advocacy of lower income taxes, and a Federal Reserve Board policy of monetary ease. But at bear market bottoms pessimism is so pervasive that there is usually a period of weeks or months before the stock market reacts to the new stimulative policies.

One reason for new stimulative policies by federal officials is that unemployment figures are high and rising, industries are not operating at full capacity, the next presidential election is two years away, and it is time to get the economy moving again. These are the signals that the bear market will end soon.

Bear markets end in an emotional panic phase during which prices often plunge dramatically in just a few days. For maximum profits the short sale should be covered during this selling-climax phase. It is usually at that point, of course, that new commitments for purchases should be made, and a new stock-price cycle begins.

Part V

The Strategy for Success

Chapter 14
Sources of Information and Ideas

Where do you look to find superperformance stocks? Many different places. I discovered Marriott (then Hot Shoppes) by dining in the company's restaurants at about the time the first public offering of stock was made in the early 1950s. I first discovered Holiday Inns when I stayed overnight in one of their motels on a trip to Florida. That was in the late 1950s and the stock was an over-the-counter security at that time.

Extensive reading or browsing in libraries sometimes brings about the discovery of a promising company. I purchased Thiokol in the mid-1950s after reading articles in technical magazines describing new developments in missile systems. Thiokol, shown on Chart 38, was one of the pioneers in the development of solid propellant motors.

Leads to many other superperformance stocks were found as a result of systematic searching. The search can be accomplished in many different ways. Here are a few of them.

Regularly review sets of long-term line charts such as those in this book. Review the charts for the various characteristics I have outlined—that is, for price volatility, expandable P/E ratios, and price and volume trends. Stocks that are undervalued compared with previous periods can be easily identified on the charts.

Publications to Review Regularly

It is important for anyone who has common stock investments also to invest a relatively small amount of money in financial publications. It is the only way to stay abreast of the latest decisions by Washington

CHART 38. THIOKOL

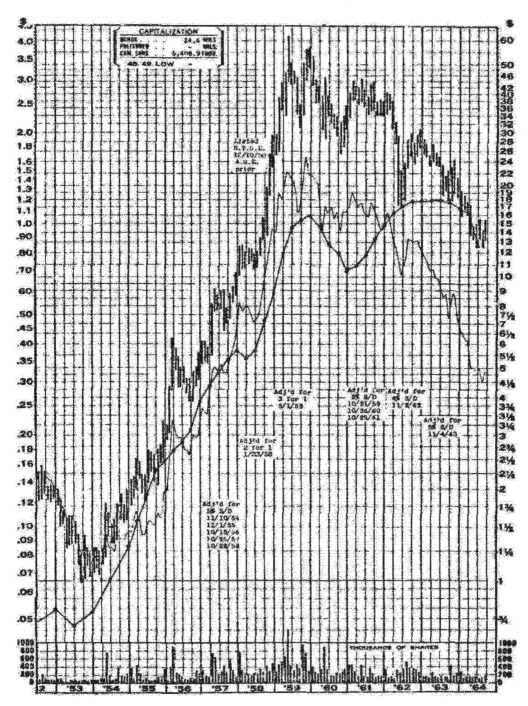

Strong earnings growth and superperformance price action
occurred for Thiokol in the 1950s as a result of the small
company's selection as contractor for solid propellant motors,
including motors for the Minuteman ICBM.

Chart by Securities Research Company

policymakers, decisions that might affect the trend of stock prices. The financial news coverage in most newspapers is unsatisfactory.

The best daily newspaper for financial and stock market news is the *Wall Street Journal,* which can be delivered to your mailbox in most sections of the country on the day of publication. The *Journal* provides a considerable amount of detailed financial information of importance to investors. This includes the daily charts of the Dow Jones industrial, transportation, and utilities averages, and tabulations of the averages by the hour. Also important are the market diary, the listings of new highs and lows, the daily percentage leaders, the most active stocks, and the digest of earnings reports. One of *the Journal's* most important contributions is that it keeps investors up to date on a daily basis.

The *M/G Financial Weekly* contains an encyclopedia of valuable information on approximately 3,450 stocks, including all stocks on the New York and American Stock Exchanges. The tabulation for each stock contains a chart and extensive data on price, volume, trend vs. the market, earnings per share, P/E ratios, dividends, shareholdings, and the financial position of each company.

The *Standard & Poor's Stock Guide,* published monthly, contains vital information on over five thousand common and preferred stocks. The *Stock Guide* gives information on each company's principal business, detailed price-range coverage, the company's financial position, capital structure and earnings record, data on dividends, and the number of institutions holding each stock, including the number of shares held. *Standard & Poor's Stock Reports,* which are detailed analyses of most publicly traded stocks, is widely respected. Standard & Poor's also publishes other valuable reference materials as well as the weekly *Outlook.*

The Value Line Investment Survey publishes a weekly *Summary of Advices and Index* containing sixteen hundred stocks in which industry groups and individual stocks are ranked on their probable market performance for the next twelve months. Value Line also estimates each stock's price range for a period of three to five years in the future. Detailed analyses of each stock are published on a rotating basis in the "Ratings and Reports"section. A weekly "Selection & Opinion" section contains information on current developments in the stock market and a stock-of-the-week selection.

Moody's is another of the large financial advisory services. Of particular value to investors is *Moody's Handbook of Common Stocks,* which is published quarterly. The volume contains reports of 1,500 stocks in tabular form and 1,010 arranged alphabetically. For each of the latter there is a chart portraying its market price history for the past twenty years and a description of the company and its business. A package of statistics and other facts on the stock are also included.

Other publications that are valuable sources of ideas are *Barren's, Business Week, Forbes, U.S. News & World Report,* and the *Wall Street Transcript.* There are many technical publications which can be of great value in providing the names of companies that are developing new products or are active in other ways that will have an important bearing on the company's growth.

Barren's contains advertising by numerous stock advisory services. The market letters of some of these services often contain important information on new developments in specific companies as well as purchase recommendations.

If you find stocks that seem worth investigating, write directly to each company for information, including copies of annual reports. You might find a prize investment.

The intelligent use of reference materials is one of the keys to success. A helpful method is to keep files and notebooks containing the names of stocks being investigated. Add to the file as important information becomes available. Then evaluate the stock and take action when the time arrives to buy stocks.

Many of my best investments have been made as a result of periodic sessions reviewing the information and evaluations in these publications of the stock advisory services. They can be found in most public libraries as well as stockbrokers' offices. Most brokers will supply customers with copies of reports on individual companies.

Learn to Recognize the Cycles

In the stock market there are repeated cycles of accumulation and advance, then distribution and decline. When the public is selling in panic at bear market bottoms, the insiders—the stock exchange specialists and other professionals—are buying. When the public is enthusiastically buying at much higher prices, the professionals are selling. It is through observing, understanding, and anticipating these buying and selling pressures that the individual investor can plan a successful investment strategy of well-timed stock purchases and sales.

Within the bull market stage of each stock-price cycle there are phases consisting of dramatically rising prices and phases in which prices are moving irregularly sideways or into decline. The most dynamic rise occurs when stock prices rebound upward from the bottom of bear markets. It is at this time, when pessimism is widespread, that large capital gains are made quickly. The new dynamic bull market is triggered because experienced professional traders realize that stocks are "sold out"—that is, anyone who might be scared into selling has already done so. The professionals conclude that they will not be surprised by additional heavy selling.

Cycles within the four-year political cycles are often caused by selling for income tax purposes. There have been many strong rallies that have started near the end of a year as selling for tax purposes was concluding. Exceptionally strong rallies began in January 1976, January 1975, December 1971, December 1970, and January 1967. Since the tax-selling cycle is dependent upon the one-year reporting period for federal income taxes, the cycle is limited in duration. Purchases made by Thanksgiving in stocks that are being sold heavily for tax purposes can often show good capital gains by February.

One question for investors to consider is to what extent the self-interest of the stockbroker, who desires to have a steady income, conflicts with that of the individual investor, whose interest is to receive a maximum return for his investment. A broker is likely to recommend a stock at any time. But my review of stock charts revealed that the best time to buy most stocks during the past fourteen years was near the bottom of the bear markets of 1962,1966,1970, and 1974. These periods lasted only a few months. It is primarily during these low-risk/high-reward periods, when the stock market is beginning to recover from a bear market, that investors should buy, and secondarily during the periods of market weakness that occur from October through December in years when there is selling to establish losses for income tax purposes.

So should we buy stocks to keep, or buy and sell with the stages of the cycles? Based on the experience of the past three decades the greater financial rewards would undoubtedly have gone to those investors who were adept at buying and selling at the right times. But not all investors have the ability or desire to buy and sell with the cycles.

Some investors do not buy at the proper time, when prices are depressed, because they fear the risk involved. They fail to perceive that risk is lessened when stock prices are depressed and that risk is increased during periods of high prices. The principal reason for their imperfect perception of risk is the news atmosphere characteristic of market troughs and tops. When stock prices are depressed there is usually a barrage of news regarding an approaching recession. Television news programs and the daily newspapers are filled with information regarding rising unemployment and declining sales and production. Usually there is an insinuation that conditions will become worse. Many investors find it psychologically difficult to buy stocks during these periods of deep pessimism.

On the other hand, declines in stock prices begin during periods of widespread optimism, when the nation is prosperous and the economy is booming. During these periods sales and production are high and little concern is voiced regarding unemployment. But it is during these periods of prosperity that investors who wish to decrease risk should sell stock.

Even astute Wall Street professionals have made bad guesses regarding which of the twin devils, recession or inflation, the Fed has decided to fight. Hundreds of millions of dollars were lost in March and April of 1974 because of plummeting bond prices, including the prices of corporate and municipal bonds and government agency issues. Bond dealers, which are banks and big securities firms, had loaded up in anticipation of higher prices. Bond prices rise when interest rates and bond yields fall; bond prices fall when interest rates and yields rise. The bond market had expected that the cost of money would decline in 1974 as a result of an easing of credit policy by the Federal Reserve and by declining demand for loans. But interest rates climbed as the demand for loans increased and the Federal Reserve Board tightened credit.

Stocks purchased for their dividend income may be particularly susceptible to Federal Reserve Board policies of monetary restraint. When the expansion of the nation's money supply slows down, credit becomes more difficult to obtain and interest rates rise. Since dividends from income-type stocks would be at a disadvantage compared with the higher bond yields, money-sensitive common stocks decline.

Look for Potential Price Movement

It is generally true that the stocks of big, mature companies with large capitalizations are not likely to decline as rapidly as the stock prices of smaller companies. However, a slow decline is more likely to cause complacency and a failure to sell at a time when the stock has gone into a price decline. The purchase of a quality stock is likely to give its purchaser a sense of security that might not be justified. In mid-September 1974, for example, IBM had declined 58 percent from its 1973 high; General Motors had declined 57 percent, Sears Roebuck 55 percent, General Electric 60 percent, and Texaco 49 percent. Some of these declines were in addition to declines from even higher prices established in the 1960s. Rather than "quality," the important thing to look for in a stock is potential price movement. Keep in mind that at some prices even the stock of the highest quality can be overpriced, and that at some prices even low-quality stocks can be underpriced.

Individual Judgment Is Crucial for Success

Common stock investment is almost entirely speculation. Today very few stocks are purchased solely for their dividends. In most cases the purchaser of common stocks is speculating that he can sell them at a higher price some time in the future—that is, for capital gains.

Traditionally, many investment counselors have believed in a buy-and-hold approach to the stock market, with safety obtained through diversification and the purchase of quality stocks. Traditionally, Wall Street has considered the speculator to be a risk taker, someone who would buy a stock today and plan to sell it in six months or a year at a higher price. It was assumed that he was willing to assume greater risk in the hope of larger gain by selecting more volatile, weaker stocks for purchase. Traditionally, Wall Street has

214

considered the investor to be a more conservative man,, an individual more interested in safety and dividend income than in taking a risk that might bring a large capital gain but might also cause the loss of the investment.

These traditional viewpoints are incorrect. Real safety lies more in the good timing of purchases and sales than in the size or the financial strength of companies selected for purchase. The stocks of many of the nation's largest companies have been in persistent downtrends for a decade or more. Among them are companies shown on charts in this book, such as AT & T, General Motors, duPont, and U.S. Steel, as well as most utilities. Conservative investors who purchased these stocks for their safety and income have suffered large losses for many years. Inflation has been taking its toll. The dividends offered by utilities and other income-type stocks have not been large enough to compete with yields from bonds, U.S. Treasury bills, certificates of deposit, and other mediums. The result has been long-term downtrends in conservative stocks. The safety feature considered so desirable did not exist. On the other hand, the well-timed purchase of carefully selected speculations has been highly rewarding to those individuals who have had the determination to spend the time and effort required to study the stock market and individual securities in a systematic manner.

The critical test in managing investments is individual judgment—the ability to interpret information correctly. An investor can have all the latest facts but if he does not have the ability to arrive at the correct conclusion, he is bound to have trouble. Generally speaking, most investors have basically the same information available to them. It is differing interpretations that cause individuals to buy different stocks, or some investors to buy the stock that others are selling.

Chapter 15
Points to Remember

The strategy to be followed for successful stock market investment can be summarized as follows:

   1. Buy when stock prices are extremely depressed following a steep decline. These periods have occurred about every four years, usually within a few months of the midpoint of a presidential term of office.

   2. Hold long positions during the uptrend in stock prices as the market recovers from depressed levels. Stock averages usually continue to rise for at least two years, although the rise for numerous individual stocks can be much shorter.

   3. Sell after stocks have had a considerable rise in price, particularly if a presidential election has been held recently—usually an indication of a possible change in national economic policy.

   4. Sell short or remain in cash as stock prices decline from high prices and as a result of federal policies. Do not re-enter the market as a buyer too soon. Wait until the selling climax has been reached.

   5. In the immediate future bear markets might not be as severe as those of 1969-70 and 1973-74 because investors are likely to be more cautious than they were in 1968 and 1972 about running up stock prices to high levels. Moreover, a large market has developed in options for people who have an urge to gamble.

   6. Future market action also depends to a large extent upon who is elected President of the United States, because federal spending policies and anti-inflation measures depend considerably on presidential positions, which vary with the individual who occupies the seat of power. But the average presidential incumbent running for re-election can be expected to follow the usual inflationary policies prior to an election,

and then tell the^ttecs: "Vote forme, I gave you prosperity."

When to Buy Stocks

To assist you in determining when to buy stocks, keep these points in mind:

    1. Follow the financial news closely to determine when the Federal Reserve switches from a restrictive monetary policy to a policy of ease.

    2. During bear markets do not buy until selling reaches the climax stage as fear-stricken investors dump their securities on the market. This occurs after market averages have declined a couple of hundred points or more over a period of at least nine months. The selling climax will consist of two hundred or more stocks making new lows for the year and no stocks making new highs. The Dow Jones industrial average will decline by twenty points or more, then suddenly rebound as professionals cover short positions and begin to reaccumulate long positions at depressed prices.

    3. The biggest stock-price gains are made when prices begin to rebound from depressed levels. In the past this has most often occurred about midway through a presidential term of office.

    4. The final test of whether a stock is a "buy" is the price action of the stock itself. Check to see if it is beginning to rebound strongly from its depressed price level.

    5. Lower than expected company earnings often cause stock prices to decline to attractive levels. This is the time to buy stocks, which will turn up as earnings return to a normal rate. But be sure to select companies that have sufficient strength and bright futures-companies that will bounce back.

    6. One of the safest times to buy is in December of years that have experienced severe bear markets. Although the selling of stocks to establish losses for tax

purposes can occur through December 31, the heaviest selling usually takes place a month or two earlier, and stock prices often have started to rebound by December. Major trend reversals occur when all the heavy selling has at last run its course.

7. The investor must be able not only to estimate future profits for a company but also to anticipate the value that the market will place on those profits, as reflected by the P/E ratio.

8. Large capital gains from common-stock investments are obtained by buying the right stock at the right time and selling it at the right time. The right time for the purchase and sale is dependent to a great extent on the stages of political cycles, which determine the timing of business and stock-price cycles.

What Stocks to Buy

To assist you in determining which stocks to buy, keep these points in mind:

1. Successful investment depends on anticipating the value that other investors will place on specific securities in future years. The most important ability for an investor to have, therefore, is the ability to forecast future trends and developments correctly.

2. Prior to purchasing a stock, review on charts its price and earnings history for the past several years. This is a quick way to gain perspective. Determine also the current price trend—whether it is down or up.

3. When stocks are rebounding from depressed price levels, the stocks most likely to rebound the fastest and the highest are those with strong prospects.

4. To determine which stocks are currently being sponsored or promoted, review the literature of investment advisory services, ask your broker for the names of stocks rated as "buys" by his company, and carefully read the financial press for stocks being favorably publicized.

5. Future earning power is one of the most important features to consider when evaluating stocks for purchase.

6. Stay up-to-date on proposed policies emanating from Washington that might affect specific securities.

7. Better investment results are usually found among dynamic small or medium-sized growth-stage companies than among the giants of industry.

8. Stocks being accumulated by institutional investors should show better results than stocks being sold on balance by institutions or those in which there is no institutional interest.

9. The potential reward is too small in most stocks most of the time to justify the risk taken by the investor with his capital.

10. Look for opportunities to make large percentage gains.

11. Do not buy a security until you have investigated and evaluated it thoroughly. Knowledge and insight are gained through careful research.

12. Whether you call it investment or speculation, keep in mind that when you buy any common stocks you are taking a calculated risk.

13. It is important that every individual who buys or is contemplating buying common stock be aware of how much of a financial risk he can afford to take. A security might look like an outstanding opportunity in all respects, but each individual must also relate the risk to his own financial situation. He should ask himself how much of a loss he can afford. Frequently a company contains only the possibility of great future growth, not the assurance of it.

When to Sell Stocks

To assist you in determining when to sell, keep these points in mind:

1. Determine the stages of the political, business,

and stock-price cycles. The strongest stock-price advances often take place during the year prior to the presidential-election year. Stock prices have frequently started to decline within a year following the presidential election.

2. Stock prices discount the future; prices move because of economic conditions expected many months ahead. Stock prices often reach their peaks before business prosperity reaches its highest levels; they rebound from their bear market lows while business is still sliding into a recession.

3. Changes in monetary policy, as announced by officials of the Federal Reserve, are strong signals of a change in the direction of stock prices.

4. News is a strong influence in the movement of stock prices. Since about five million people read the *Wall Street Journal* every day, information and articles in that newspaper can and often do have an effect on prices.

5. When good news no longer pushes up the price of a stock, the stock might be a sell candidate.

6. Determine if the downside risk is greater than the potential profit.

7. When the upward momentum of a stock's price has slowed or stopped, consider whether the stock should be sold.

8. Ask yourself if you would be willing to buy the security at its present price. If you would not be willing to buy, why expect someone else to?

9. Stocks do not all reach their final high prices simultaneously. Some might top out several months prior to the final top in the market averages.

10. A goal of many institutional investors-continuous, uninterrupted growth—is unrealistic. The real world consists of cycles.

11. Stock prices do not just decline; many are forced down by heavy short selling on the part of professional traders.

12. Stockbrokers have a strong bullish bias.

Pessimism is considered to be bad for their business. Their optimism could sometimes be bad for your investments.

13. Stocks should not be purchased and then forgotten. To remain long in stocks during a bear market is not only illogical, but also expensive. Re-examine your positions often.

14. Most losses result from the market's assigning lower P/E multiples rather than from any fundamental company change, such as lower earnings.

15. Stock prices move because of expectations, and the P/E ratio measures those expectations.

16. A high rate of inflation often precedes a decline in stock prices and a downturn in the national economy. Businessmen and consumers react to rising costs and prices by cutting back on spending. The sharp reduction in demand results in lower levels of production and increasing unemployment. As pessimism grows, consumers become even more cautious about spending. Recessions develop and stock prices continue to decline until confidence is restored.

Appendix A
Superperformance Stocks
1962-74

The following stocks experienced Superperformance price action during the period from mid-1962 to 1974. The time span of each Superperformance phase and the percentage increase in the price of the stock are shown. Most of the stocks that had Superperformance action are included, but the list should not be considered all-inclusive. In addition, numerous stocks were eliminated because price reactions exceeding 25 percent occurred during the Superperformance action. To qualify as a Superperformance stock, the price had to increase at least 300 percent in a minimum of two years.

AAV Companies
400% August 1966-December 1968

ACF Industries
300% June 1962-November 1964

Adams-Millis
700% September 1966-October 1967

Admiral
800% January 1965-April 1966

Aileen
1200% October 1966-January 1969

Airwick
600% January 1971-August 1972

Alaska Interstate
300% November 1971-April 1972

Alberto Culver
400% September 1966-August 1967

Alcon Laboratories
300% May 1f70-February 1973

Allegheny
400% July 1970-April 1971

Allegheny Airlines
400% January 1965-April 1966

Alien Group
400% December 1966-January 1968

Allied Maintenance
400% December 1966-June 1968

Allied Products
300% January 1965-May 1965
300% June 1965-March 1966

Ambac Industries
400% October 1966-October 1967

Amcord
300% January 1967-August 1968

Amerada Hess
300% July 1965-May 1966
400% October 1966-November 1968
300% May 1970-June 1971

American Airlines
300% October 1962-March 1964

American Building Maintenance Industries
800% February 1967-July 1968
300% June 1970-March 1972

American District Telegraph
300% May 1970-March 1972

American Express
450% May 1970-January 1973

American Greetings
400% June 1970-July 1972

American Hospital Supply
300% October 1966-June 1968

American Medical International
1500% November 1966-October 1967
400% March 1968-January 1969
300% May 1970-March 1971

American Petrofina
500% August 1966-May 1969

American Safety Equipment
400% September 1964-May 1965

American Standard
300% October 1966-December 1968

Ametek
300% January 1967-September 1967

AMF
400% May 1970-April 1972

Amrep
2000% January 1967-May 1969
300% July 1970-February 1971

Angelica
300% March 1968-April 1969

Ansul
300% December 1964-February 1966

Anthony Industries
1200% December 1966-May 1969
800% August 1971-July 1972

Apache
500% November 1966-June 1968

APL Corp.
300% August 1964-October 1964
400% November 1966-June 1967

Archer-Daniels-Midland
300% April 1972-September 1973

Asamera Oil
400% March 1965-April 1965
500% November 1968-June 1969

Athlone Industries
1200% October 1966-December 1968

Atlas
300% December 1966-August 1967

A-T-O
300% November 1966-January 1968

Automated Building Components
400% December 1966-December 1968
300% June 1970-April 1971

Automatic Data Processing
1400% August 1965-December 1967
300% March 1968-January 1970

Avco
300% January 1967-August 1967

Avery Products
800% November 1965-January 1970

Avnet
500% October 1966-December 1967

Aztec Oil & Gas
300% June 1970-July 1971

Babcock & Wilcox
300% June 1970-April 1971

Baker Oil Tools
500% May 1970-December 1972

Bally Manufacturing
1200% December 1970-November **1972**

Bangor Punta
300% October liiB-JSttuVVy t@6l

224

Banister Continental
300% July 1970-February 1971
400% November 1971-December
1972

Bath Industries
500% December 1966-June 1968
700% July 1970-April 1972

Bausch & Lomb
600% July 1970-January 1972
300% April 1973-October 1973

Baxter Laboratories
700% July 1964-September 1967

Belco Petroleum
400% October 1966-November
1967

Benguet Consolidated
600% February 1967-February
1968

Berkey Photo
300% November 1963-April 1964
300% June 1965-April 1966

Blessings
400% May 1964-April 1965

Block (H & R)
1400% October 1966-December
1968

Boeing
500% July 1963-January 1966

Boise Cascade
500% October 1966-May 1968

Braniff International
1500% January 1964-June 1966

Browning Ferris
300% December 1970-April 1972

Brunswick
500% July 1970-April 1972

Bucyrus-Erie
500% November 1963-February
1966

Bunker Ramo
300% October 1918-duMs 1967

Burndy
400% October 1964-April 1966

Burns International Security Services
600% October 1966-October 1968

Burnup & Sims
1200% July 1970-January 1973

Burroughs
300% May 1965-August 1966
500% October 1966-January 1970

Buttes Gas & Oil
1200% December 1966-February
1969

Caldor
400% July 1970-February 1972

California Computer Products
600% October 1966-July 1967

Campbell Chibougamau Mines
300% August 1965-April 1966

Capital Cities Communications
300% January 1964-January 1966
300% May 1970-March 1972

Carlisle
400% July 1965-July 1967

Castle & Cooke
300% July 1966-December 1968

Cerro
300% November 1962-November
1964

Certain-Teed Products
400% July 1970-May 1972

Champion Home Builders
1000% December 1967-May 1969
2600% July 1970-July 1972

Chelsea Industries
900% January 1967-August 1968

Chicago Bridge & Iron
1000% June 1970-November 1973

Chicago Milwaukee
500% October 1962-November 1964

Chock Full O'Nuts
300% December 1966-December 1967

Chromalloy-American
300% June 1965-February 1966

Chrysler
600% June 1962-September 1964

City Investing
500% October 1966-January 1968

Clark Oil & Refining
700% October 1964-June 1966
300% March 1968-June 1969

Clorox
500% June 1970-January 1973

CMI Investment
300% April 1968-August 1968
600% May 1970-May 1972

Coastal States Gas
900% October 1966-March 1970

Coca-Cola Bottling (N.Y.)
450% February 1970-August 1972

Cole National
700% October 1966-December 1968

Coleman
450% October 1967-January 1970

Collins & Aikman
300% May 1970-March 1972

Colt Industries
600% October 1966-May 1968

Columbia Broadcasting System
300% October 1962-May 1964

Columbia Pictures Industries
400% September 1966-June 1968

Communications Satellite
300% May 1970-April 1971

Compugraphic
500% November 1971-July 1972

Computer Sciences
800% October 1966-December 1967

Conrac
350% October 1966-January 1968

Consolidated Freightways
300% July 1970-January 1972

Continential Airlines
400% November 1962-March 1964
400% January 1965-September 1966

Continental Mortgage Investors
600% October 1966-May 1969

Control Data
400% December 1962-December 1963
600% October 1966-October 196?

Cook United
400% December 1966-November 1968

Cooper Laboratories
300% April 1968-January 1969

Cordura
700% October 1966-December 1967
400% March 1968-December 1969

CTS Corp.
300% December 1964-March 1966

Culligan International
400% October 1962-September 1964

Curtiss-Wright
500% December 1971-July 1972

Cutler-Hammer
300% July 1970-August 1971

Cyprus Mines
400% August 1964-February 1966

Dayco
300% October 1966-January 1968

DeKalb Agresearch
300% June 1970-July 1971
300% November 1971-January 1973

Delta Airlines
400% May 1962-March 1964
400% January 1965-April 1966

Deltona
300% December 1966-January 1988
700% April 1968-October 1969

Dennison
500% October 1962-January 1964
300% October 1966-December
1967
300% July 1970-July 1971

Denny's
600% October 1966-January 1968
300% March 1968-December 1968

Deseret Pharmaceutical
300% September 1966-November
1967
300% November 1971-January
1973

Diebold
300% March 1968-February 1970

Digital Equipment
500% October 1966-December
1967

Dillingham
700% December 1966-September
1968

Disney
300% October 1966-December
1967

Dr. Pepper
300% October 1962-April 1964
400% December 1966-October
1968
400% May 1970-April 1972

Dome Petroleum
400% June 1966-July 1967
300% August 1970-July 1971

Duplan
1700% December 1966-December
1968

Eckerd (Jack)
400% May 1964-February 1966
1000% November 1966-October
1969
300% May 1970-September 1971

E G & G
600% May 1966-October 1967

Ehrenreich Photo-Optical Ind.
300% August 1965-March 1966
600% December 1966-December
1968

Emery Air Freight
300% October 1964-June 1966

Englehard Minerals & Chemicals
600% January 1967-July 1968

Esquire
1000% September 1964-March 1967

Ethan Alien
900% June 1970-March 1972

Ethyl
400% June 1963-January 1965

Evans Products
700% January 1963-April 1965

Faberge'
400% May 1966-March 1968

Fairchild Camera
900% December 1964-February
1966

Fansteel
400% October 1966-July 1967

Far West Financial
300% March 1968-August 1968

Fedders
1000% December 1966-November
1968

**Federal National Mortgage
Association**
300% July 1970-January 1972

Federal Sign & Signal
300% October 1966-March 1968

Ferro
300% August 1970-August 1972

Financial Federation
300% December 1967-September
1968

First Charter Financial
350% September 1966-April 1967

Fischbach & Moore
300% January 1967-December
1968

Fisher Foods
450% December 1966-January 1968
400% April 1968-February 1969

Fleetwood Enterprises
2400% January 1967-December 1968
700% May 1970-April 1972

Flexi-Van
500% September 1967-November 1968
300% July 1970-March 1972

Fluor
400% June 1964-January 1966
300% October 1966-June 1967

Flying Tiger
450% June 1965-April 1966
300% October 1966-July 1967
400% July 1970-April 1971

Foster Wheeler
300% October 1966-July 1967
300% December 1972-January 1974

Franklin Mint
300% July 1968-February 1969
400% September 1970-April 1971

Fuqua
500% July 1966-June 1967

GAF
350% July 1970-March 1972

Gannett
400% June 1970-August 1972

Garan
1100% November 1966-December 1968
600% June 1970-January 1972

GCA Corp.
400% October 1966-September 1967

General Cable
550% October 1962-April 1966

General Cinema
800% June 1967-December 1968
300% May 1970-April 1971

General Development
900% October 1966-May 1969

General Instrument
550% September 1964-August 1966

Genuine Parts
450% May 1970-May 1972

Georgia-Pacific
350% October 1966-December 1968

Giant Food
350% October 1966-November 1968

Giddings & Lewis
350% October 1966-June 1967

Gino's
2400% December 1966-November 1969
300% August 1970-June 1972

Global Marine
450% June 1966-January 1968

Gordon Jewelry
350% September 1964-March 1966
700% October 1966-December 1968

Grainger
400% June 1970-December 1972

Gray Drug Stores
300% April 1964-January 1966
350% December 1966-November 1968

Great Lakes Chemical
300% October 1966-April 1967

Greyhound
300% June 1962-April 1964

Grumman
300% June 1964-February 1966

Guardian Industries
400% December 1971-May 1972

Gulf Resources
450% June 1965-March 1966
300% September 1966-August 1967

228

Gulf & Western Industries
500% June 1964-April 1966
300% October 1966-February 1967
300% May 1970-April 1971

Gulton Industries
300% June 1965-June 1966
350% October 1966-December 1967

Halliburton
500% May 1970-January 1973

Handleman
400% October 1966-January 1968

Harland (John H.)
500% May 1970-April 1972

Heller (Walter E.)
300% December 1966-October 1968

Helmerich & Payne
400% October 1966-January 1968

Hewlett-Packard
300% August 1964-April 1966
450% July 1970-January 1973

High Voltage
300% September 1962-September 1963

Hilton Hotels
900% October 1966-November 1968

Hoffman Electronics
300% August 1970-March 1971

Holiday Inns
400% October 1966-December 1967

Home Oil
350% August 1968-May 1969
400% May 1970-September 1971

Hoover
350% May 1962-March 1964

Horizon
2100% October 1966-October 1969
350% July 1970-December 1970

Howard Johnson
500% July 1970-May 1972

Howmet
900% April 1965-October 1967

Huffman Manufacturing
300% November 1967-February 1969

Humana
500% February 1968-December 1968

Huyck
900% September 1966-January 1970

Hygrade Food Products
400% March 1968-December 1968

ICN Pharmaceutical
900% December 1966-January 1968

Imperial Corporation of America
300% December 1967-March 1968

Imperial Oil
300% May 1970-December 1972

Interco
350% October 1966-July 1968

International Flavors and Fragrances
1300% June 1962-July 1966

International Minerals & Chemical
470% October 1962-February 1966

International Rectifier
500% May 1965-April 1966

Interstate United
600% June 1967-November 1968

Iowa Beef Processors
300% July 1965-February 1966

Ipco Hospital Supply
300% October 1966-January 1968

Itek
300% April 1963-January 1964
300% July 1965-August 1966

Japan Fund
400% March 1968-May 1969

Jim Walter
800% October 1966-December 1968

Johnson & Johnson
300% May 1970-May 1972

Johnson Products
300% May 1970-December 1970

Josten's
300% December 1966-May 1968

Joy
650% October 1962-February 1966

Kaiser Industries
300% October 1966-January 1968

Katy Industries
600% December 1966-January 1968

Kaufman & Broad
2600% October 1966-March 1970

Kawecki Berylco
300% October 1966-June 1967

King's Department Stores
400% December 1966-May 1968
300% June 1970-May 1971
300% June 1963-March 1965

KLM Royal Dutch Airlines
400% August 1965-March 1966

Knight Newspapers
350% July 1970-August 1972

Kresge (S.S.)
300% September 1963-December 1965
400% January 1967-October 1969
450% July 1970-January 1973

Lafayette Radio Electronics
400% October 1966-June 1968
400% May 1970-July 1971

Lear Siegler
300% December 1964-April 1966

Leaseway Transportation
650% August 1970-June 1972

Leslie Fay
500% June 1964-April 1966

Lenox
500% January 1967-February 1969

Levitz Furniture
1300% May 1970-May 1972
300% July 1968-December 1968

Loews
200% October 1966-January 1968
300% July 1970-July 1971

Longs Drug Stores
400% December 1966-December 1968
400% May 1970-February 1972

LTV Corp.
600% October 1966-August 1967

Lubrizol
300% December 1966-December 1968

Lucky Stores
700% October 1966-April 1971

Lykes-Youngstown
300% June 1967-May 1968

Madison Square Garden
400% October 1966-July 1967

Magnavox
300% June 1965-April 1966

Malone & Hyde
300% May 1970-June 1972

Mapco
300% October 1966-October 1968
450% July 1970-January 1973

Marathon Manufacturing
500% November 1967-January 1969

Marcor
300% December 1967-June 1969

Maremont
1300% July 1970-November 1972

Marion Laboratories
800% October 1966-October 1968
350% July 1970-July 1972

Marley
1000% April 1965-June 1968
300% July 1970-April 1972

Marriott
400% August 1966-December 1968
350% July 1970-May 1972

Mary Kay Cosmetics
300% August 1971-January 1973

Masco
600% November 1966-October 1968
400% May 1970-April 1972

Massey Ferguson
300% November 1962-November 1964

Mattel)
1300% December 1966-September 1968

Mav Department Stores
300% July 1970-January 1972

McCulloch Oil
400% January 1967-August 1967
450% May 1970-April 1971

McDermott (J. Ray)
600% May 1964-May 1968

McDonald's
500% October 1966-December 1967
750% September 1970-December 1972

McDonnell Douglas
300% October 1966-July 1967
300% July 1970-March 1971

Me Lean Trucking Company
400% October 1966-February 1969

Melville Shoe
400% October 1966-December 1968

Menasco
800% October 1966-December 1967
300% July 1970-February 1971
300% November 1971-August 1972

Metro-Goldwyn-Mayer
400% July 1965-October 1967

Metromedia
300% October 1962-October 19^3;
300% July 1970-March 1971

MGIC Investment
1100% December 1966-May 196i
800% May 1970-January 1973

Microdot
600% October 1966-September 1967

Microwave Associates
300% June 1965-August 1965
600% October 1966-October 1967

Milgo Electronics
300% March 1968-June 1968
350% November 1971-May 1972

Milton Bradley
600% October 1966-June 1968
900% May 1970-June 1972

Mobile Home Industries
1000% May 1970-April 1972

Mohasco Industries
300% July 1970-April 1972

Mohawk Data Sciences
2200% December 1965-December 1967

Monarch Machine Tool
300% December 1966-November 1967

Monroe Auto Equipment
900% October 1966-March 1970
300% July 1970-March 1972

Motorola
700% October 1962-March 1966

Murphy Oil
350% November 1971-October 1973

Murray Ohio Manufacturing
400% October 1966-April 1969

Nashua
400% October 1966-December 1968

National Airlines
1800% June 1962-April 1966

National Chemsearch
400% June 1970-January 1973
500% October 1966-January 1968

National Semiconductor
400% July 1973-October 1973
800% October 1966-September
1967

National Union Electric
450% December 1964-April 1966
300% December 1970-August 1971

Natomas
800% April 1968-May 1969
500% May 1970-September 1970

New England Nuclear
700% May 1970-August 1972

New Process
900% December 1966-November
1969
700% May 1970-January 1972

Norris Industries
350% October 1966-July 1967
400% July 1970-March 1972

Northrup. King
300% November 1971-June 1972

Northwest Airlines
2000% October 1962-June 1966

Northwest Industries
1300% October 1962-April 1966
400% June 1970-April 1972

Norton Simon
300% December 1966-January
1968

Occidental Petroleum
450% October 1966-November
1967

Ogden
400% October 1966-January 1968

Outboard Marine
450% July 1970-March 1972

Overnight Transportation
300% October 1966-June 1968
700% May 1970-September 1971

Pacific Petroleums
500% October 1966-June 1969

Pan American World Airways
500% October 1962-April 1964
300% July 1965-June 1966

Papercraft
300% August 1966-January 1968

Pargas
350% December 1963-March 1965

Pasco
400% October 1963-April 1965
400% October 1966-November
1967
300% July 1970-October 1970

Peabody Galion
450% April 1968-March 1969
800% May 1970-July 1972

Perm-Dixie Industries
300% October 1966-October 1967

Pennzoil
400% October 1963-April 1965
350% October 1966-June 1968

Perkin-Elmer
450% November 1970-June 1972

Petrie Stores
550% May 1970-January 1973

Philip Morris
500% May 1970-January 1973

Phillips Industries
2000% November 1966-December
1968

Pickwick International
1500% September 1966-May 1969
350% July 1970-May 1972

Pittston
300% July 1969-April 1971

Pizza Hut
500% August 1971-January 1973

Polaroid
500% June 1964-August 1966

Ponderosa System
4500% May 1970-June 1972

Quaker State Oil Refining
450% October 1962-March 1966
400% August 1970-December
1972

Ramada Inns
400% December 1966-January 1968
300% May 1970-July 1971

Ranco
300% June 1967-December 1968

Raymond International
500% October 1966-August 1968

Reading & Bates Offshore Drilling
700% October 1962-April 1965
300% May 1970-September 1970

Reliance Group
1400% October 1966-December 1968

Research-Cottrell
300% November 1967-May 1968
500% May 1970-May 1972

Reserve Oil and Gas
400% January 1967-January 1968

Resistoflex
300% October 1966-October 1967

Revco D. S.
500% August 1966-July 1968
300% May 1970-April 1972

Rite Aid
1000% May 1970-April 1972

Robins (A. H.)
350% November 1970-January 1973

Rockower Brothers
800% June 1967-May 1969

Rohm & Haas
400% July 1970-February 1973

Rohr Industries
300% June 1964-December 1965

Rollins
1000% March 1964-April 1965
500% October 1966-November 1968
300% July 1970-July 1972

Rorer-Amchem
300% October 1966-May 1968

Rosario Resources
500% November 1971-March 1974

Royal Crown Cola
300% October 1970-December 1971

Royal Industries
400% September 1963-February 1966
400% August 1966-July 1967

Russ Togs
300% October 1966-June 1968
300% July 1970-March 1971

Ryder System
600% October 1966-February 1969
300% October 1970-August 1972

Ryan Homes
300% May 1970-April 1972

St. Joe Minerals
300% October 1962-January 1965

Sanders Associates
500% August 1965-July 1966
650% November 1966-December 1967

Sangamo Electric
300% January 1965-December 1965
300% October 1966-November 1967

Sante Fe International
450% June 1966-November 1968
300% May 1970-April 1971

Sav-A-Stop
500% August 1964-February 1966
350% October 1967-November 1969

Savin Business Machines
700% April 1968-April 1969

Saxon Industries
550% December 1965-June 1966
300% September 1966-June 1967
300% March 1968-December 1968

Schlitz (Jos.) Brewing
300% November 1970-November 1972

Schlumberger
400% January 1967-September
1969
800% May 1970-December 1973

SCM Corp.
500% June 1965-April 1966

Scott and Fetzer
500% June 1970-May 1972

Scott Foresman
300% June 1964-June 1966

Scovill
500% October 1962-April 1966

Seaboard Coast Line Industries
300% July 1970-October 1971

Seaboard World Airlines
350% June 1965-April 1966

Searle (G.D.)
300% July 1970-July 1972

SEDCO
600% July 1970-November 1972

Seven-Up
300% April 1968-March 1970

Servomation
300% June 1970-October 1971

Sheller-Globe
300% December 1963-April 1965

Simmons Precision Products
2500% February 1965-April 1966

Simplicity Pattern
300% October 1966-October 1967

Skaggs Companies
500% October 1966-October 1968

Skyline
900% November 1962-September
1963
2100% January 1967-December
1968
400% May 1970-October 1971

Smith International
1000% August 1964-December
1968

Sony
400% July 1965-March 1966
600% January 1968-November
1969
450% November 1971-January
1973

Southland
350% January 1967-December 1968

Southwest Forest Industries
450% January 1968-April 1969

Spencer
550% April 1968-January 1969

Sperry Rand
300% October 1966-December
1967

Sprague Electric
400% June 1965-January 1967

Standard Brands Paint
650% December 1966-February
1970
400% May 1970-February 1972

Stokely-Van Camp
350% December 1966-Octobe
1967

Sundstrand
800% July 1965-December 1967

Sunshine Mining
350% December 1963-September
1964

Supermarkets General
300% April 1964-February 1966
300% May 1970-September 1971

Superscope
500% October 1966-June 1967

Syntex
2100% October 1962-January 1964
350% June 1965-February 1966
600% July 1970-March 1972

Systran Donner
300% October 1966-December
1967

Taft Broadcasting
300% January 1964-JarHjary 1068
300% July 1970-March Is971

Talley Industries
450% February 1965-July 1966
400% October 1966-September
1967

Tandy
300% July 1964-May 1965
500% November 1966-January
1968
300% March 1968-November 1969
300% July 1970-February 1972

Tappan
300% December 1967-December
1968
350% July 1970-April 1972

Technicolor
300% October 1962-October 1963
400% January 1967-July 1967

Teledyne
400% July 1965-June 1966
500% October 1966-October 1967

Teleprompter
300% October 1966-May 1967

Telex
300% October 1966-August 1967
1700% April 1969-January 1970

Tesoro Petroleum
400% March 1968-December 1968

Texasgulf
400% July 1963-April 1964

Texas Instruments
700% October 1962-August 1966

Texas Oil & Gas
400% September 1966-April 1968

Textron
900% October 1962-December
1967

Tidewater Marine Service
1000% December 1962-December
1964
300% August 1970-March 1971

Time
500% October 1962-December
1965

Tokheim
300% December 1966-June 1968
300% December 1971-July 1972

Tonka
900% October 1966-May 1968

Town & Country Mobile Homes
800% March 1967-September 1968

Transamerica
350% October 1966-December
1968

Trans World Airlines
750% October 1962-March 1965
300% November 1970-April 1971

Transcon Lines
300% July 1970-December 1971

TRE Corp.
500% August 1966-February 1967
700% August 1970-February 1972

Tropicana Products
1400% May 1970-May 1972

Twin Fair
1000% October 1966-February
1968

Tyco Laboratories
750% November 1966-January 1968
300% November 1971-January 1972

Tyler
500% August 1970-April 1972

UAL
350% September 1964-April 1966
350% July 1970-April 1971

Unarco
300% June 1964-June 1965

United Aircraft
350% February 1964-January 1966

United Brands
1000% December 1966-January
1968

United Financial of California
300% September 1966-February
1967
300% December 1967-September
1968

United Nuclear
400% October «66-October 1967

United Piece Dye Works
800% November 1962-August 1963
1000% October 1966-May 1968
700% May 1970-March 1971

U.S. Filter
400% June 1965-January 1966
300% October 1966-May 1967

U.S. Industries
400% October 1966-January 1968

U.S. Leasing
400% October 1966-December 1967
450% August 1970-March 1972

U.S. Radium
750% March 1964-November 1965

Unitrode
300% December 1970-May 1972

Upjohn
600% May 1970-August 1973

Uris Buildings
500% December 1966-May 1969

UV Industries
400% June 1962-February 1963
350% August 1965-April 1966

Valley Metallurgical Processing
1100% July 1965-February 1966
500% October 1966-August 1967

Varian Associates
400% June 1964-April 1966

Vetco Offshore Industries
500% May 1970-April 1971
400% August 1971-December 1973

Victor Comptometer
350% April 1964-October 1965

Vornado
500% December 1964-April 1966
300% May 1970-March 1971

Wackenhut
300% December 1966-December 1967

Ward Foods
350% December 1965-February 1966
600% October 1966-December 1968

Watkins-Johnson
600% October 1966-July 1968
300% July 1970-March 1971

Webb (Del E.)
700% December 1966-May 1969

Wells, Rich, Greene
500% August 1970-March 1971

Western Airlines
650% May 1962-May 1964
500% July 1970-April 1971

Wheelabrator-Frye
400% October 1966-August 1968

White Consolidated Industries
1000% December 1963-August 1966

Williams
1100% February 1964-January 1966
400% October 1966-January 1968
300% May 1970-April 1971

Winnebago Industries
1200% December 1970-April 1972

Wyly
3700% October 1966-November 1968

Xerox
700% June 1962-October 1964

XTRA
1400% November 1964-April 1966
600% October 1966-June 1968

Yates
450% March 1968-March 1969

Zale
600% December 1966-December 1968

Zapata
1100% April 1963-July 1966
700% October 1966-July 1968
300% July 1970-July 1971

Zayre
800% February 1964-October 1965

Zurn
700% November 1966-May 1968

236

Appendix B
Superperformance Stocks
October 1974-October 1976

During the two-year period following the bear market lows of October and December 1974 there were 243 stocks that had superperformance price action by tripling or more. The stocks were:

Abbott Laboratories
Adams-Millis
Addressograph-Multigraph
Aileen
Airco
Akzona
Alaska Interstate
Alien Group
Allied Stores
Allis-Chalmers
Ambac
Amcord
American Air Filter
American Airlines
American Bakeries
American Building Maintenance
American Family
American Seating
American Standard
Ampex
Anthony Industries
APL Corp.
Archer-Daniels-Midland
Arlen Realty & Development
Asamera Oil
Atlas
Automatic Data Processing

Avco
Baker Industries
Bangor Punta
Beckman Instruments
Beech Aircraft
Bendix
Big Three Industries
Blue Bell
Boise Cascade
Brockway Glass
Burns International Security Services
Burndy
Burnup & Sims
Caldor
Capital Cities Communications
Centronics Data Computer
Chemetron
Cluett, Peabody
CNA Financial
Coleman
Collins & Aikman
Columbia Pictures
Combustion Equipment Associates
Compugraphic
Computer Sciences
Congoleum
Conrac

Consolidated Freightways
Cook United
Cooper Industries
Crane
Crouse-Hinds
CTSCorp.
Cubic
Curtiss-Wright
Dana
Dart Industries
Data General
Dayton Hudson
Denny's
Deseret Pharmaceutical
Diamond Shamrock
Digital Equipment
Disney (Walt) Productions
Eagle-Pichet
Easco
Eastern Gas and Fuel Associates
Edison Brothers Stores
EMI Ltd.
Envirotech
Ethan Alien
Evans Products
Fairchild Camera & Instrument
Falcon Seaboard
Farah
Fedders
Federal Signal
Fieldcrest Mills
First Charter Financial
Fisher Scientific
Fleetwood Enterprises
Fluor
Fort Howard Paper
Franklin Mint
GCA Corp.
General Cinema

General Development
General Dynamics
General Instrument
General Medical
General Signal
Gerber Products
Gino's
Gray Drug Stores
Great Lakes Chemical
Gulf & Western
Gulf Resources and Chemical
Gulton Industries
Hanes
Hanna Mining
Harris
Heublein
Hilton Hotels
Holiday Inns
Hospital Corporation of America
Host International
House of Fabrics
Houston Natural Gas
Houston Oil & Minerals
Howard Johnson
Humana
Imperial Corporation of America
International Rectifier
Iowa Beef Processors
Ipco Hospital Supply
Itek
Itel
Jim Walter
Jonathan Logan
Joy Manufacturing
Kane Miller
Kaufman & Broad
Kidde (Walter)
Koehring
Koppers

238

Leaseway Transportation'
Leesona
Levi Strauss
Levitz Furniture
Litton Industries
Lockheed Aircraft
Lykes
Macy (R. H.)
Magic Chef
Mapco
Maremont
Marley
May Department Stows
MCA
McCord
McKee (Arthur G.)
McLean Trucking
Melville
Menasco Manufacturing
Merrill Lynch
Mervyn's
Metro-Goldwyn-Mayer
Metromedia
Microwave Associates
Midland-Ross
Milgo Electronics
Milton Bradley
Mobile Home Industries
Moore McCormack Resources
Narco Scientific Industries
National Medical Care
National Semiconductor
Neptune International
New Process
Norris Industries
Northrop
Northwest Airlines
Norton Simon
NVF Co.

Occidental Petroleum
Olin
Pan American World Airways
Pay Less Drug Stores Northwesl
Petrolane
Philips Industries
Pickwick Internationa,
Pittston
Pizza Hut
Ponderosa System
Purolator
Raymond International
RCA
Research-Cottrell
Revco D.S.
Rexnord
Riegel Textile
Rio Grande Industries
Rite Aid
Rockower Brothers
Rollins
Ryan Homes
Ryder System
St. Joe Minerals
Sambo's Restaurants
Sanders Associates
Savin Business Machines
Scott & Fetzer
Seaboard World Airlines
Seligman & Latz
Seven-Up
Sheller-Globe
Simmonds Precision PrraiJudiS
Skaggs
Smith International
Superscope
Tandy
Tektronix
Teledyne

Teleprompter
Telex
Tiger International
Tokheim
TRE Corp.
Trinity Industries
Tropicana Products
TRW
Twentieth Century-Rax Film
Tyco Laboratories
United Brands
United Nuclear
United Refining
U.& Filter
U.S. Shoe
United Technologies

Univar
Valley Industries
Valmac Industries
Varian Associates
Viacom International
Wallace-Murray
Wal-Mart Stores
Warner Communications
Watkins-Johnson
Wheelabrator-Frye
White Consolidated
Woolworth (F. W.)
Yellow Freight System
Zayre
Zenith Radio
Zurn Industries

9 798210 365514